THE AUSSIE BBQ BIBLE

THE AUSSIE BBQ BIBLE

100+ RECIPES FOR THE GREAT OUTDOORS

OSCAR SMITH

CONTENTS

INTRO
page 8

CHICKEN
page 16

PORK
page 38

SEAFOOD
page 62

LAMB
page 80

BEEF
page 96

VEGGIE
page 112

SIDES & SALADS
page 132

DESSERTS
page 168

INDEX
page 184

INTRO

This book is your guide to getting the absolute best out of your barbecue – whether it's a modest charcoal bucket or a gas-burning beast with all of the bells and whistles – we've got the best recipes to please a crowd.

Here you'll find more than a 100 recipes designed for cooking in the great outdoors. We've covered all the important barbecuing food groups – chicken, beef, lamb, pork, fish and seafood, as well as options for vegetarian mains.

But what's a steak or a barbecued leg of lamb without something delicious to go with it? So, in this book you'll also find a huge selection of salads and sides to go with your meaty (or non-meaty) mains. We haven't forgotten dessert either – you'll also find sweet recipes that work a treat on the barbecue.

So fire-up and get cooking!

EQUIPMENT

HERE ARE SOME OF THE ESSENTIAL – AND NOT-SO ESSENTIAL (BUT DEFINITELY HANDY TO HAVE) – BITS AND PIECES FOR GETTING THE MOST OUT OF YOUR BARBECUE.

LONG-HANDLED METAL TONGS
Your most important tool. Any metal tongs will do, but it's best to avoid light-weight aluminium ones as they will bend out of shape and tend to heat up more easily.

GRILL BRUSH
For cleaning. You want a brush with stiff metal bristles. If you have a hotplate look for a brush that has a scraper attached to it as well.

METAL SPATULA
Essential for turning burgers and delicate fish.

MEAT THERMOMETER
The secret to perfectly-cooked meat. There are plenty of different types available at prices to suit any budget, but for barbecuing, I'd definitely recommend a digital thermometer as they give you an instant read.

BASTING BRUSH
For adding all-important flavour during cooking. Brushes with silicone bristles are much easier to clean than the traditional-style ones, and a long handle is preferable to keep your hands from the heat.

METAL SKEWERS
They're reusable, they don't burn and they don't require soaking. Stainless steel is best, and ensure the skewer is slightly oval or square, as it grips the food better. Just remember that they do get hot!

PIZZA STONE
Once you make a pizza in your barbecue, you'll never go back. A pizza stone works especially well in a kettle-shaped cooker as the domed top reflects the heat perfectly.

FISH BASKET
Two wire frames connected by a hinge on one side that can be closed over food and then turned and moved easily using the handles. Brilliant for cooking whole fish.

SMOKER BOX
A great way to get that smoky-flavoured goodness even when cooking with gas.
A simple cast-iron or stainless-steel box that you fill with soaked woodchips and place on top of the barbecue. (It's also simple to create a smoke box using foil.)

CHOOSING THE RIGHT BBQ

THERE ARE TWO MAIN CAMPS WHEN IT COMES TO OUTDOOR BARBECUING: GAS OR CHARCOAL. BOTH HAVE THEIR BENEFITS AND DRAWBACKS, SO IT'S IMPORTANT TO KNOW WHICH WILL BEST SUIT YOUR REQUIREMENTS.

CHARCOAL
There is just no substitute for the distinctive smoky flavour you get from cooking on charcoal. Charcoal barbecues can also reach higher temperatures than gas barbecues, allowing for direct, searing heat for perfectly-charred steaks that stay rare in the middle. That said, charcoal is messy to handle, it requires much more forethought and lighting time (you'll need to light your charcoal 30–45 minutes beforehand) and charcoal is more expensive and less commonly-available than gas canisters (especially if you're using good-quality hardwood charcoal). But if convenience is not your main priority, then charcoal barbecuing is an extremely rewarding way to go.

GAS
Quick, clean and easy, the convenience of a gas barbecue is hard to beat. A gas barbecue lights instantly with no other materials required (as long as your gas bottle is full) and usually only takes about 10 minutes to heat. Gas barbecues also hold their temperatures more steadily and are easy to clean. Some say cooking on gas is a less 'authentic' experience, but if you appreciate the ease of getting home from work, lighting up your barbecue and having dinner cooked in 15 minutes with no fuss, then a gas barbecue is a fantastic option.

SIZE
It's important to consider your requirements and available space when buying a barbecue. There's no sense buying an eight-burner behemoth if you've only got a small balcony to put it on, whereas if you're likely to be regularly cooking for crowds (and have the space) you probably want to consider something on the larger scale.

HOOD
It's absolutely worthwhile getting a barbecue with a hood or lid. It makes for a much more versatile piece of equipment, allowing you to cook low and slow, roast vegetables or larger pieces of meat, and even hot-smoke fish or ribs.

DURABILITY
This doesn't (always) mean you have to spend a fortune, but, especially if your barbecue is not going to live undercover, make sure it's made from durable materials. Get yourself a cover if the barbecue is likely to get wet when it rains.

EXTRAS
If you're willing to pay for them, there's a cornucopia of additional features and add-ons available to the outdoor cook. Some are gimmicks, but a few legitimately useful extras you might look out for are:

- **A rotisserie:** wonderful for slow, even cooking, especially whole chickens or a boneless leg of lamb.

- **Warming racks:** useful if you're cooking for a crowd or if you're barbecuing a variety of meats or vegetables with different cooking times.

- **A light**: speaks for itself, really. Who hasn't had to pull out their phone torch to check if the sausages are done?

- **An internal thermometer:** great if you're planning on roasting or cooking at low temperatures.

- **A wok burner:** definitely something to consider if you don't have a gas stovetop in your kitchen.

LOOKING AFTER YOUR BBQ

THERE'S NO SENSE IN SPENDING GOOD MONEY ON YOUR BARBECUE TO NOT KEEP IT IN THE BEST CONDITION YOU CAN. IT DOESN'T TAKE MUCH TIME OR EFFORT TO KEEP IT IN GREAT SHAPE FOR THE YEARS OF COOKING TO COME.

TIPS FOR CLEANING

- **Clean your barbecue after every use:** barbecues are much easier to clean when warm, so, once you're done eating, turn the heat back on for a few minutes. Turn the burners off and give the hotplate and grill a good scrape with a metal brush to dislodge any food or grease. If there's an excess of grease, use paper towel or newspaper to soak it up.

- **Avoid harsh chemicals:** after all – your food is going on there! Edible acids like lemon juice and vinegar are great for cutting grease. Fill a spray bottle with a 1:1 mixture of water and white vinegar and keep it handy for cleaning.

- **Don't forget the outside of the barbecue:** absorbent wipes (such as BBQ wipes) are handy to keep the outside of the barbecue looking as good as the inside. Remember – looking after your barbecue now will reward you with many more years of cooking.

MAINTENANCE

- **Do a deep-clean:** every month or two, take the grates and/or hotplate out, soak in hot soapy water and give everything a good scrub. You should wear dishwashing gloves when doing this as it will allow you to use hotter water, which helps to cut through grease.

- **Routinely check for gas leaks:** with the gas turned on, run a little soapy water along the gas line and connections. If the water bubbles, there's a leak, and you need to either tighten the connection or replace the line.

- **Keep it covered:** it's well worth getting a cover, especially if your barbecue is exposed to the elements, including excessive sunshine and rain.

- **Replace the fat absorber pellets regularly:** if you have a drip tray, line it with aluminium foil and fill it with fat absorber pellets (you'll find these at specialist barbecue stores). These collect the fat drippings from the barbecue plates, reduce odour and prevent fat fires from occuring.

HOW TO TELL WHEN YOUR MEAT IS COOKED

THE BEST WAY TO ENSURE PERFECTLY-COOKED MEAT EVERY TIME IS TO USE A MEAT THERMOMETER. IF YOU'RE RESTING MEAT BEFORE SERVING (WHICH IS DEFINITELY RECOMMENDED), REMEMBER THAT THE INTERNAL TEMPERATURE WILL RISE DURING THAT TIME, SO REMOVE THE MEAT FROM THE HEAT A LITTLE BIT BEFORE IT REACHES YOUR DESIRED TEMPERATURE.

CHICKEN
Chicken needs to be completely cooked through and never eaten rare. Chicken is cooked when the internal temperature reaches 75°C. When cooking a whole bird, a meat thermometer should be inserted into the thickest part of the thigh. If you don't have a meat thermometer, pierce the same part of the thigh with a sharp knife – if the juices run clear then the chicken is cooked. If they're pink or red then the chicken needs to be cooked a little longer.

PORK
For many years, pork had to be overcooked to be deemed safe for consumption, but stricter health regulations over the past few decades means pork can now be enjoyed at its best: medium, still with a little blush of pink in the middle. Pork is medium when the internal temperature is at 71°C.

LAMB
Lamb can be eaten rare, especially lean cuts like backstrap or tenderloin, but is generally at its best somewhere between medium-rare and medium (45–55°C).

BEEF
As beef is perfectly delicious eaten raw, ideal internal temperature is entirely up to personal preference (and your desired outcome). For best results you shouldn't go much above 60°C as the meat will start to dry out.

THE COOKING GUIDE

CHICKEN	
COOKED	75°C

PORK	
MEDIUM	71°C
WELL-DONE	77°C

LAMB	
RARE	35°C
MEDIUM-RARE	45°C
MEDIUM	55°C
MEDIUM-WELL	65°C
WELL-DONE	75°C

BEEF	
RARE	35°C
MEDIUM-RARE	45°C
MEDIUM	55°C
MEDIUM-WELL	65°C
WELL-DONE	75°C

CHICKEN

BARBECUED PERI PERI CHICKEN
page 18

BRAZILIAN CACHAÇA CHICKEN SKEWERS
page 21

GRILLED BUTTERMILK CHICKEN
page 22

TENNESSEE BEER CAN CHICKEN
page 24

APPLE CIDER CHICKEN DRUMSTICKS
page 25

BARBECUED CHICKEN BURGERS WITH BASIL AIOLI
page 27

FIERY LEMONGRASS CHICKEN WINGS
page 28

BUTTERFLIED CHICKEN WITH ROSEMARY OIL
page 31

BBQ BUFFALO WINGS WITH BLUE CHEESE DIP
page 32

LEMON & GARLIC WINGS
page 33

SPICY SATAY CHICKEN SKEWERS
page 34

CHIPOTLE CHICKEN BURRITOS
page 37

BARBECUED PERI PERI CHICKEN

SERVES 4–6

1.4 kg whole chicken, butterflied, skin patted dry with paper towel
crusty bread, to serve
Portuguese salad (page 149), to serve (optional)

PERI PERI SAUCE

5 fresh long red chillies
5 garlic cloves, unpeeled
1 teaspoon dried oregano
1 teaspoon sweet paprika
1 teaspoon soft brown sugar
80 ml (⅓ cup) olive oil
50 ml cider vinegar
1½ teaspoons salt

To make the sauce, first preheat the oven to 220°C. Place the chillies on a baking tray and roast for 10 minutes. Set aside to cool then roughly chop. Meanwhile, blanch the garlic cloves in boiling water for 30 seconds, then peel and roughly chop. Combine with the chilli and the remaining ingredients in a small saucepan over medium heat and simmer for 2–3 minutes. Allow the mixture to cool, then puree in a blender.

Place the chicken on a tray and coat with the peri peri sauce, reserving some sauce for basting. Cover with plastic wrap and refrigerate for at least 1 hour.

Preheat a hooded barbecue grill to medium and lightly grease with oil.

Place the chicken skin-side down on the grill and cook, covered, for 7–8 minutes. Turn and cook the other side, basting. Continue to cook with the hood closed, turning and basting occasionally, for a further 30 minutes until cooked through.

Serve with crusty bread and, if you like, a side of Portuguese salad.

BRAZILIAN CACHAÇA CHICKEN SKEWERS

SERVES 4–6

1 kg skinless chicken thigh fillets, each cut into 3 pieces
bamboo skewers, soaked in cold water
baby cos lettuce leaves, to serve
½ cup coriander leaves
¼ cup mint leaves
1 lime, cut in half

CACHAÇA MARINADE

2 tablespoons olive oil
60 ml (¼ cup) cachaça (see note)
juice of 1 lime
zest of 2 limes
2 garlic cloves, crushed
1 cup mint leaves, torn
1 long red chilli, finely chopped
½ teaspoon paprika
1 teaspoon soft brown sugar
1 teaspoon sea salt flakes

To make the marinade, combine the ingredients in a mixing bowl.

Add the chicken pieces to the marinade, stirring well to coat. Cover the bowl in plastic wrap (or transfer the whole lot to a zip-lock bag) and refrigerate for at least 4 hours or overnight.

Preheat a barbecue grill to medium and lightly grease with oil.

Thread the chicken pieces onto the skewers and cook on the grill, turning occasionally, for about 6–8 minutes until cooked through.

Pile the lettuce leaves onto a serving platter and place the skewers on top. Scatter with the coriander and mint leaves, and squeeze the lime juice over the top.

Note: Cachaça is a popular Brazilian distilled spirit made from sugarcane juice. Locally it may be referred to as 'holy water', 'heart opener' and 'tiger breath'. It is available at large liquor outlets. This recipe is best started a day ahead to allow the sensational bold flavours to develop.

GRILLED BUTTERMILK CHICKEN

SERVES 4–6

500 ml (2 cups) buttermilk
4 garlic cloves, crushed
2 teaspoons wholegrain mustard
2 teaspoons hot paprika
3 teaspoons sea salt flakes
1 teaspoon freshly ground black pepper
2 sprigs rosemary, leaves roughly chopped
1.4 kg whole chicken, cut into quarters
lemon halves, to serve
green salad and Barbecued potato wedges with lime yoghurt (page 140), to serve (optional)

Combine the buttermilk, garlic, mustard, paprika, salt, pepper and rosemary in a mixing bowl.

Place the chicken in a large zip-lock bag and pour in the buttermilk mixture. Ensure the chicken pieces are well coated. Refrigerate for at least 8 hours or overnight, turning the bag occasionally to disperse the marinade.

Preheat a hooded barbecue grill to medium and lightly grease with oil.

Remove the chicken from the marinade and drain. Place the chicken onto the grill skin-side down, cover and cook for 20 minutes, turning once after 10 minutes. Turn again and cook for another 5–10 minutes until the chicken is cooked through.

Serve with lemons halves and, if desired, a simple green salad and Barbecued potato wedges.

TENNESSEE BEER CAN CHICKEN

SERVES 4

1.4 kg whole chicken
1 tablespoon olive oil
375 ml (1½ cups) can lager-style wheat beer
Barbecued potato wedges with lime yoghurt (page 140), to serve (optional)

SPICE RUB

2 teaspoons sweet paprika
2 teaspoons smoked paprika
2 teaspoons soft brown sugar
1 teaspoon ground cumin
½ teaspoon ground coriander
½ teaspoon garlic powder
1 teaspoon sea salt flakes

Preheat a hooded barbecue grill to medium–low and lightly grease with oil.

To make the spice rub, mix the ingredients together in a small bowl.

Coat the chicken in olive oil, and season well with the spice rub mix.

Open the beer can and pour out about a third of the beer. Place the cavity of the chicken over the can, legs down, so that the chicken sits upright. Place carefully on the grill, close the lid and cook for about 1½ hours, until the chicken is cooked through. The chicken is done when a meat thermometer placed into the thickest part of the thigh reads 75°C at minimum, or the juices run clear when pierced with a skewer.

Remove the chicken carefully from the grill and set aside to rest for 20 minutes before removing the can and carving. For a great match, serve with Barbecued potato wedges.

APPLE CIDER CHICKEN DRUMSTICKS

SERVES 4

8 chicken drumsticks
1 long red chili, thinly sliced
½ cup mint leaves

APPLE CIDER MARINADE
250 ml (1 cup) apple cider
2 tablespoon peanut oil
2 tablespoons light soy sauce
2 garlic cloves, crushed
2 cm piece ginger, grated
1 fresh red chilli, chopped finely
zest of 1 lemon
¼ teaspoon white pepper

To make the marinade, combine the ingredients in a medium-sized bowl.

Place the drumsticks in a large zip-lock bag. Pour in the marinade and seal, pressing out any excess air. Massage to ensure the chicken is well coated with the marinade, and refrigerate for 4 hours, turning occasionally to evenly distribute the marinade.

Remove the chicken from the refrigerator 30 minutes before cooking to allow to come to room temperature.

Preheat a barbecue grill to medium and lightly grease with oil.

Place the chicken on the grill, cover and cook, turning regularly, for 15 minutes or until cooked through and juices run clear when the meatiest part of the drumstick is pierced with a skewer.

Serve on a platter garnished with the sliced chilli and mint leaves.

Barbecued Chicken Burgers with Basil Aioli

SERVES 4

4 round wholemeal buns, split
1 avocado, mashed
1 cup rocket leaves
1 large tomato, sliced

CHICKEN BURGERS

500 g minced chicken
1 garlic clove, finely chopped
¼ cup basil leaves, torn
½ cup flat-leaf parsley leaves, finely chopped
1 teaspoon dried chilli flakes
1 teaspoon sea salt flakes
½ teaspoon freshly ground black pepper
zest and juice of 1 lemon
2 tablespoons dry breadcrumbs
1 egg, lightly beaten

BASIL AIOLI

2 egg yolks, at room temperature
2 garlic cloves, finely chopped
½ teaspoon sea salt flakes
2 tablespoons lemon juice
½ cup basil leaves, roughly chopped
185 ml (¾ cup) mild-flavoured olive oil

To make the burgers, combine the ingredients in a large mixing bowl. Mix well using your hands until you can see the herbs are evenly dispersed. Using wet hands, shape the mixture into patties slightly larger than the round of the buns. Place the patties on a plate lined with baking paper and cover with plastic wrap. Refrigerate for 1 hour.

To make the aioli, place the egg yolks, garlic, salt, lemon juice and basil in a food processor and pulse until well combined and creamy. With the motor running, add the oil in a thin, steady stream and keep processing until the mixture thickens. Taste and adjust the seasoning. Refrigerate until needed.

Preheat a barbecue hotplate to medium and lightly grease with oil.

Cook the burgers for about 4–5 minutes on each side or until cooked through. Place the buns, cut-side down, on the hotplate to lightly toast. Allow the buns to cool slightly before spreading avocado on the base of each bun, then top with rocket, a chicken burger and a slice of tomato. Dollop the aioli generously on the tomato then top with the remaining bun halves.

Note: The basil aioli recipe makes about 250 ml (1 cup). Any remaining aioli can be used on burgers or as a dip for wedges or crudites. It will keep in an airtight container in the fridge for up to 1 week.

Fiery Lemongrass Chicken Wings

SERVES 4

1 kg chicken wings
¼ cup coriander leaves
1 bird's eye chilli, finely sliced

MARINADE

2 lemongrass stalks, white part only, finely chopped
2 bird's eye chillies, finely sliced
4 coriander roots and stems, washed and finely chopped
4 garlic cloves, finely chopped
2 tablespoons soft brown sugar
1 teaspoon ground turmeric
2 tablespoons peanut oil
juice of 2 limes
2 tablespoons soy sauce
60 ml (¼ cup) fish sauce

To make the marinade, pound the lemongrass, chilli, coriander and garlic to a paste using a mortar and pestle. Add the sugar and turmeric and mix well. Add the peanut oil, lime juice and sauces, and stir to combine.

Transfer the marinade to a dish that will comfortably fit the chicken wings. Add the chicken and coat well. Cover with plastic wrap and refrigerate for at least 2 hours, or overnight.

Preheat a barbecue grill to medium–low and lightly grease with oil.

Place the chicken wings on the grill and cover with the hood. Cook, turning occasionally, for 25–30 minutes until the marinade has caramelised and charred and the chicken is cooked through.

Pile the wings onto a platter and garnish with the coriander leaves and sliced chilli.

BUTTERFLIED CHICKEN WITH ROSEMARY OIL

SERVES 4–6

1.5 kg whole chicken, butterflied, skin patted dry with paper towel
2 lemons, halved

ROSEMARY OIL

¼ cup fresh rosemary leaves, finely chopped
zest of 1 lemon
2 garlic cloves, roughly chopped
¼ teaspoon black pepper
¾ teaspoon sea salt flakes
2 tablespoons olive oil

To make the rosemary oil, pound the rosemary, lemon zest, garlic, pepper and salt to a paste using a mortar and pestle. Add the oil and mix well.

Rub the rosemary oil all over the chicken, coating the skin and underside well. Reserve a tablespoon of the oil for basting.

Cover the chicken with plastic wrap and set aside for 30 minutes to bring it to room temperature.

Preheat a hooded barbecue grill to medium–high and lightly grease with oil.

Place the chicken skin-side down on the grill, cover and reduce heat to low. Cook for 20 minutes, baste the underside with a sprig of rosemary or a basting brush, then turn the chicken over and baste the skin side. Cover and cook for a further 20 minutes.

If the skin requires further browning and crisping, baste the skin side again and turn over to cook until browned.

Remove from the heat, cover loosely with foil and rest for 10 minutes before carving. Serve with lemon for squeezing over.

BBQ BUFFALO WINGS WITH BLUE CHEESE DIP

SERVES 4

75 g (½ cup) plain flour
½ teaspoon cayenne pepper
½ teaspoon garlic powder
½ teaspoon salt
1 kg chicken wings
125 ml (½ cup) melted butter
125 ml (½ cup) American-style hot sauce (such as Crystal or Tabasco)

BLUE CHEESE DIP

150 g blue cheese
250 g sour cream
juice of ½ lemon
1 tablespoon white vinegar
salt and freshly ground black pepper

Combine the flour, cayenne pepper, garlic powder, and salt in a dish that will comfortably fit the chicken wings. Add the chicken and toss to coat well. Cover with plastic wrap and refrigerate for at least 1 hour.

Preheat a barbecue grill to medium-low and lightly grease with oil.

Whisk together the melted butter and hot sauce. Dip the wings into the butter mixture, and place on a tray.

Place the chicken wings on the grill and cover with the hood. Cook, turning occasionally, for 25–30 minutes until the outside has caramelised a little and the chicken is cooked through.

Meanwhile, to make the blue cheese dip, mash the cheese to a paste using a fork then combine with the other ingredients in a small bowl. Taste and season with salt and pepper.

Pile the wings onto a platter and serve with the dip alongside.

LEMON & GARLIC WINGS

SERVES 4

1 tablespoon olive oil
4 garlic cloves, crushed
200 ml lemon juice
salt and freshly ground pepper
1 kg chicken wings
1 lemon, finely sliced
1 small handful coriander leaves, finely chopped
1 teaspoon nigella seeds
Greek yoghurt, thinned with a little water, to serve

Combine the olive oil, garlic and lemon juice in a dish that will comfortably fit the chicken wings and season generously with salt and pepper. Add the wings and lemon slices and coat well. Cover and refrigerate for at least 2 hours or overnight.

Preheat a barbecue grill to medium–low and lightly grease with oil.

Place the chicken wings on the grill and cover with the hood. Cook, turning occasionally, for 25–30 minutes until the outside has caramelised a little and the chicken is cooked through.

Pile the wings onto a platter, sprinkle with the coriander and nigella seeds and drizzle with a little yoghurt.

SPICY SATAY CHICKEN SKEWERS

SERVES 4

600 g chicken thigh fillets, cut evenly into 3 cm strips
bamboo skewers, soaked in cold water
iceberg lettuce leaves, to serve
cucumber slices, to serve
½ fresh pineapple, cut into chunks

MARINADE

2 lemongrass stalks, white part only, thinly sliced
2 garlic cloves, roughly chopped
2 teaspoons finely grated palm sugar
1 teaspoon ground coriander
1 teaspoon ground cumin
1 teaspoon ground turmeric
1 tablespoon peanut oil

PEANUT SAUCE

200 g raw unsalted peanuts
12 dried red chillies, deseeded
2 lemongrass stalks, white part only, finely chopped
3 French shallots, finely chopped
2 garlic cloves, finely chopped
1 tablespoon ground coriander
2 teaspoons finely grated palm sugar
60 ml (¼ cup) peanut oil
1 tablespoon tamarind paste
1 tablespoon kecap manis
125 ml (½ cup) coconut milk

To make the marinade, pound the lemongrass and garlic into a paste using a mortar and pestle. Add the palm sugar, coriander, cumin, turmeric and oil, and mix well.

Transfer the marinade to a bowl, add the chicken and mix well. Cover with plastic wrap and refrigerate for at least 4 hours or overnight.

To make the sauce, first preheat the oven to 180°C. Spread the peanuts on a baking tray and roast for about 5 minutes until fragrant and lightly golden. Set aside to cool, then finely chop. Meanwhile, soak the chillies in hot water for 15 minutes. Drain and roughly chop. Place the chilli into a food processor along with the lemongrass, shallots, garlic, coriander, sugar and peanut oil and process until a paste forms. Heat a medium-sized saucepan over medium heat and add the chilli paste. Cook, stirring continuously for 5 minutes. Add 500 ml (2 cups) of water and bring to the boil, then add the tamarind, kecap manis, peanuts and coconut milk. Simmer for 5 minutes over low heat or until thickened.

Preheat a barbecue grill to medium-high and lightly grease with oil.

Thread 3–4 chicken pieces onto each skewer so that the chicken lies fairly flat. Cook on the grill, turning regularly, for 3–4 minutes until slightly charred and cooked through. (Cooking time will be determined by the thickness of the chicken.)

Arrange the lettuce, cucumber, pineapple and skewers onto plates. Serve with a small bowl of sauce for each person.

CHIPOTLE CHICKEN BURRITOS

SERVES 4

500 g chicken tenderloins, trimmed
2 corn cobs
4 burrito tortillas
400 g tinned black beans, rinsed and drained
½ iceberg lettuce, shredded
½ cup coriander leaves

CHIPOTLE MARINADE

1 tablespoon chipotle chillies in adobo sauce, chopped
2 tablespoons honey
3 garlic cloves, crushed
2 teaspoons sea salt

FRESH TOMATO SALSA

3 ripe tomatoes, diced
½ red onion, finely diced
1 fresh jalapeño chilli, finely chopped
¼ cup coriander leaves, chopped
1 avocado, diced
½ teaspoon salt
juice of ½ lime

CHIPOTLE AIOLI

2 egg yolks, at room temperature
¼ teaspoon sea salt flakes
juice of ½ lemon
1 small garlic clove, crushed
2 tablespoons chipotle chillies in adobo sauce, chopped
250 ml (1 cup) mild-flavoured olive oil

To make the marinade, combine the ingredients in a medium-sized bowl. Add the chicken, and mix to coat well. Cover with plastic wrap and refrigerate for 1 hour.

To make the salsa, combine the tomato, onion, chilli, coriander and avocado in a medium-sized bowl. Add the salt and lime juice and mix well.

To make the aioli, place the egg yolks, salt, lemon juice, garlic and chipotle into a small food processor. Process on low and add the oil in a thin, steady stream until incorporated.

Preheat a barbecue grill to high and lightly grease with oil.

Grill the corn, turning occasionally, for about 8–10 minutes until well blackened all over. Remove and set aside to cool. Remove the kernels from the cobs using a sharp knife.

Reduce the grill heat to medium. Cook the chicken for about 10 minutes or until cooked through, turning every 3 minutes. The honey will make the chicken more likely to burn, so frequent turning is important.

To assemble the burritos, first warm the tortillas for 5–10 seconds on the grill. Top each burrito with chicken, salsa, corn, beans, lettuce and coriander, and then drizzle with the chipotle aioli. (The key to wrapping a burrito is to not overfill, so make sure no more than a third of the tortilla is covered.) Fold in both sides, and then roll the tortilla to contain the filling.

Note: The aioli recipe makes about 375 ml (1½ cups). Any remaining aioli can be used on burgers or as a dip for the Barbecued potato wedges on page 140. It will keep in an airtight container in the fridge for up to 1 week.

PORK

PORK TENDERLOIN WITH MAPLE, GINGER & ORANGE GLAZE
page 40

ASPARAGUS WRAPPED IN BACON
page 42

CHERRY TOMATO & BACON SKEWERS
page 43

HOMEMADE PORK & FENNEL SAUSAGES
page 46

HOMEMADE PORK & VEAL SAUSAGES
page 47

GRILLED PORK RIBS WITH VIETNAMESE DIPPING SAUCE
page 49

HOMEMADE BRATWURST
page 50

CURRYWURST
page 51

SOUTHERN-STYLE BABY BACK PORK RIBS
page 52

BACON-WEAVE CHEESEBURGERS
page 54

BACON WRAPPED MAC & CHEESEBURGERS
page 55

SMOKEY CHIPOTLE BARBECUED PORK RIBS
page 58

JAMAICAN JERK PORK BELLY
page 59

KOREAN BARBECUED PORK
page 61

Pork Tenderloin with Maple, Ginger & Orange Glaze

SERVES 4

zest and juice of 2 oranges
80 ml (⅓ cup) apple cider vinegar
5 cm piece ginger, peeled and finely grated
2 teaspoons dijon mustard
1½ teaspoons smoked paprika
1½ teaspoons sea salt flakes
1 tablespoon olive oil
2–3 pork tenderloins (about 600 g in total)
125 ml (½ cup) pure maple syrup
Chargrilled witlof (page 145), to serve (optional)

In a small saucepan, combine the orange zest and juice, vinegar, ginger, mustard, paprika and salt. Simmer over medium–low heat for 3–4 minutes. Set aside to cool.

Transfer 60 ml (¼ cup) of the marinade to a large zip-lock bag along with the oil. Add the pork and seal, pushing out as much of the air as you can. Massage the marinade into the pork and place in the refrigerator for at least 1 hour.

Meanwhile, add the maple syrup to the remaining marinade in the saucepan to make the glaze. Simmer for 4–5 minutes until reduced and thickened slightly. Reserve half the glaze for serving.

Preheat a barbecue grill to medium-high and lightly grease with oil.

Cook the pork for 2 minutes each side until browned all over. Reduce the heat to medium-low and cook, turning and basting with the glaze, for a further 10–12 minutes or until cooked through.

Cover the pork and rest for 5 minutes.

Cut the pork into 1 cm slices and spoon the reserved glaze over the top. If desired, serve with Chargrilled witlof.

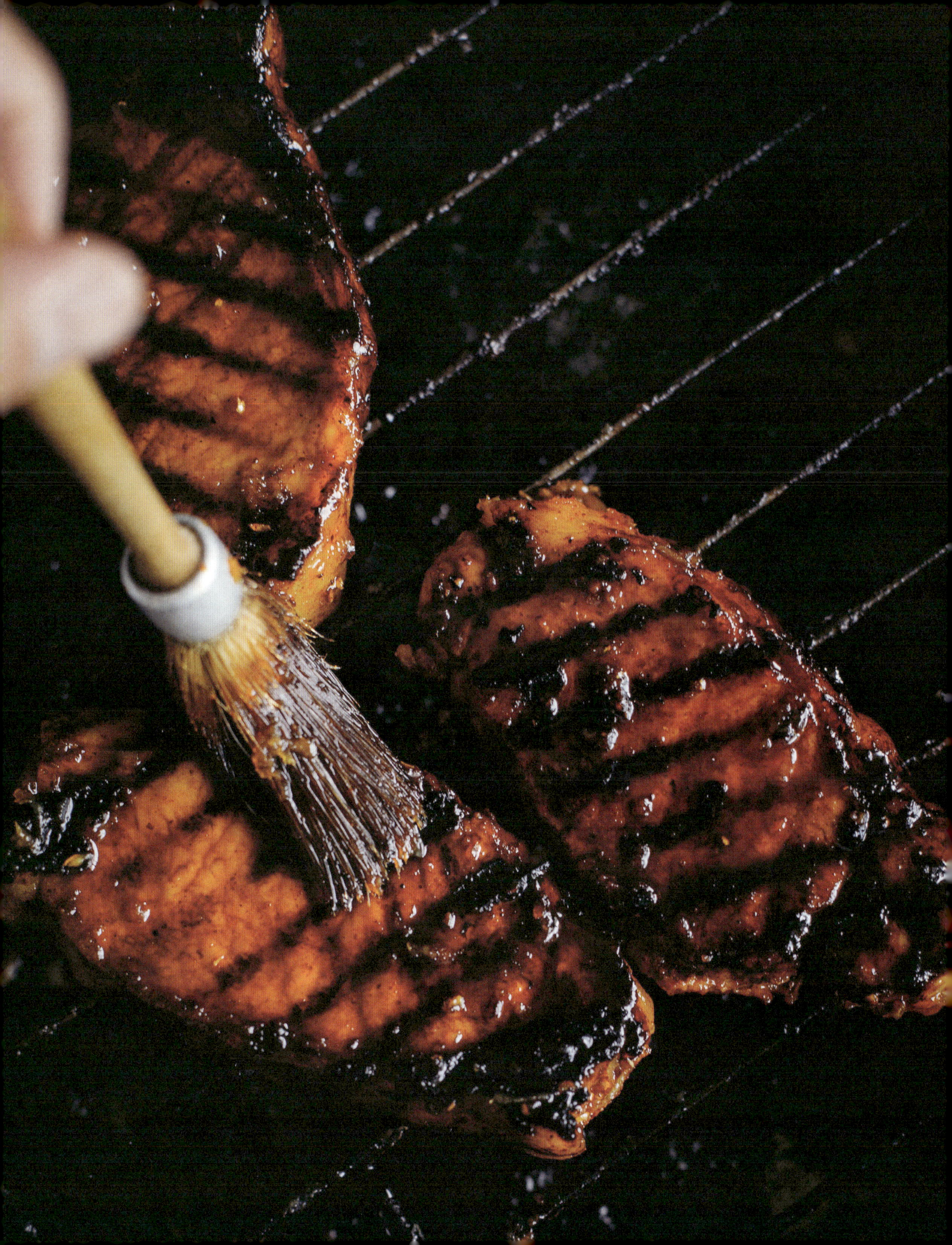

ASPARAGUS WRAPPED IN BACON

SERVES 4

2 bunches asparagus, ends trimmed
4 slices rindless streaky bacon
olive oil, for drizzling
1 tablespoon brown sugar
1 tablespoon toasted black sesame seeds

Preheat a barbecue grill to medium.

Divide the asparagus into four bundles. Wrap each bundle with a slice of bacon and secure with a piece of kitchen string. Drizzle with a little olive oil.

Cook the asparagus, turning carefully every now and then, for 6–8 minutes or until the asparagus is lightly charred and the bacon is cooked through. Sprinkle all over with sugar and cook for a further 1–2 minutes until the sugar is caramelised.

Serve immediately scattered liberally with the sesame seeds and seasoned with pepper.

CHERRY TOMATO & BACON SKEWERS

SERVES 4

250 g cherry tomatoes

250 g haloumi, cut into cubes

4 bamboo skewers, soaked in warm water for 30 minutes

4 slices rindless streaky bacon, cut in half lengthways

Preheat a barbecue grill to medium.

Thread the cherry tomatoes and haloumi alternately onto the skewers, weaving the bacon on the skewer between the pieces. You will need two strips of bacon per skewer. If there is bacon left over at the end of each skewer, just keep threading it on.

Cook the skewers, turning carefully every now and then for 8–10 minutes until the haloumi is lightly charred and the bacon is cooked through. It's important not to have the barbecue or chargrill too hot as the bacon needs a chance to cook through before the tomatoes and cheese.

Season with a little salt and pepper to serve.

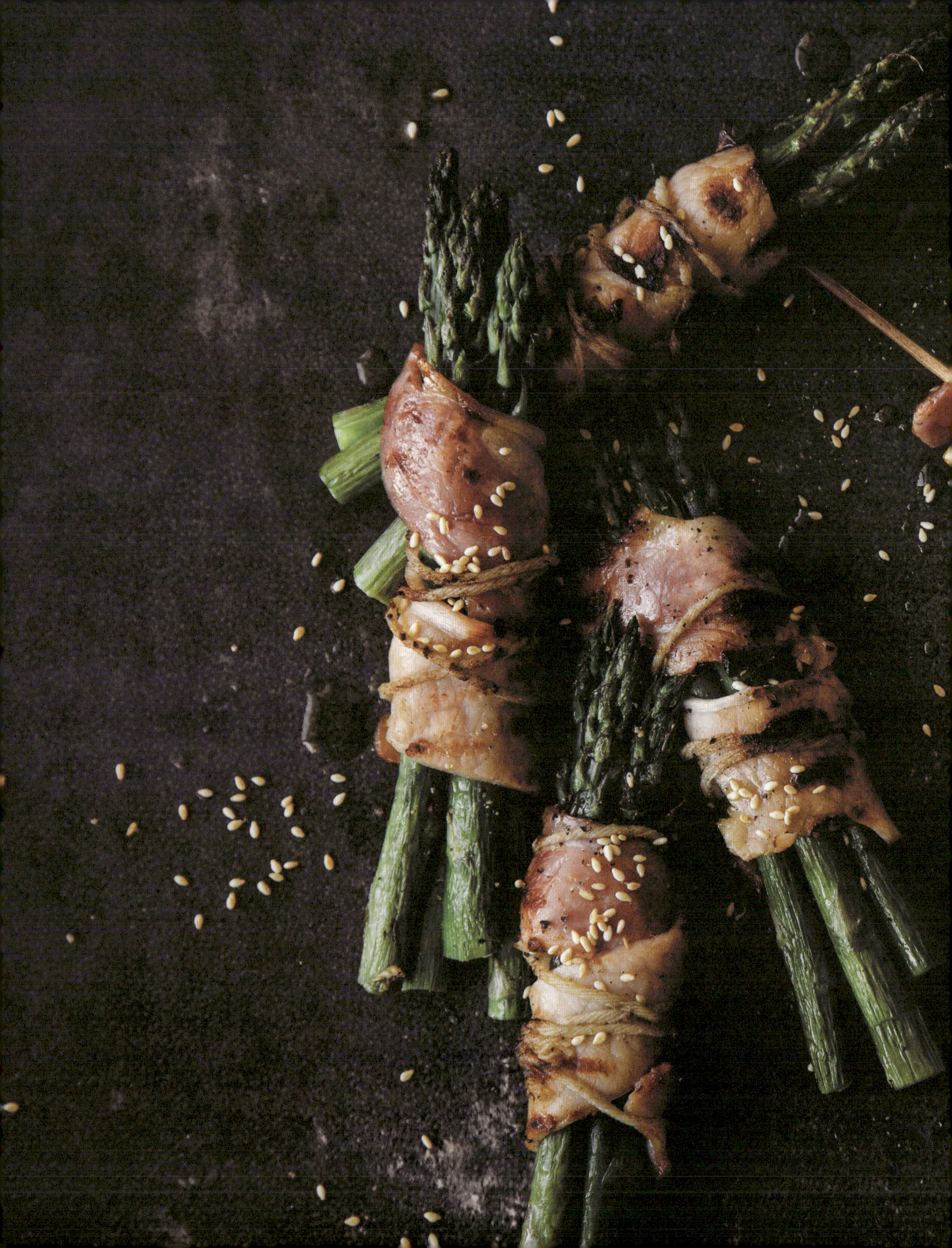

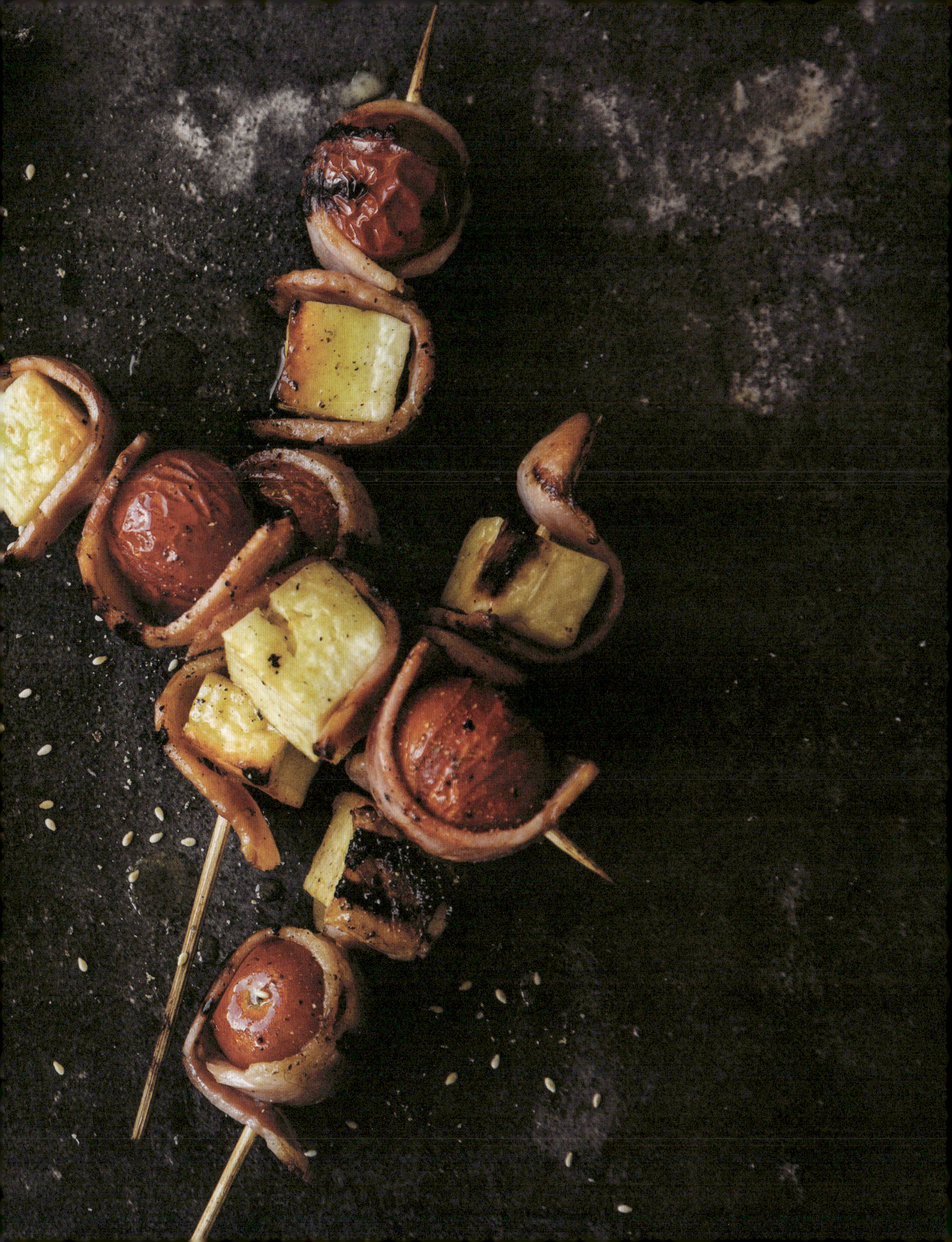

Homemade Pork & Fennel Sausages

MAKES 1 KG

2 tablespoons fennel seeds
1 kg minced pork, at least 30% fat content (see note)
1 tablespoon ground black pepper
1 tablespoon salt
2 teaspoons dried chilli flakes (optional)
60 ml (¼ cup) chilled dry white wine
natural sausage casings (see note)

Note: Sausage casings can be ordered through your local butcher. Natural casings are best. Casings are stored salted so must be rinsed inside and out with cold water before use.

Note: You can ask your butcher to mince your choice of cut for sausages – scotch fillet, shoulder and belly pork are all ideal. A fairly coarse grind and a minimum of 30% fat will give you the best result.

Toast the fennel seeds in a small dry frying pan over medium heat until fragrant. Transfer to a large mixing bowl and add the pork, pepper, salt and chilli flakes (if using). Using your hands, mix well until the mixture becomes sticky. (This is an important step as it will improve the final texture.) Add the wine and continue to mix.

The flavouring can be checked at this stage by cooking a spoonful of pork mixture in a small frying pan with a little olive oil over medium–high heat. Taste and adjust the seasoning if necessary.

Run cold tap water through the sausage casing until the water runs clean. Cut a length of casing about 2 metres long and feed the casing onto the nozzle of a sausage maker. Leave a bit of casing hanging over to allow any excess air to escape. Feed the mince through the machine or nozzle, assisting the casing to slide off the nozzle as it is filled. Press out any air bubbles. Tie the end in a knot, and working towards the untied end, twist the filled casing into sausage lengths. Tie the open end in a knot. (If you don't have a sausage maker you can make the sausages by hand using a wide-necked funnel.)

Place the sausages onto a plate and cover with a clean tea towel. Refrigerate overnight or up to 48 hours before cooking (this allows the flavours to develop and also reduces the likelihood of the skins splitting).

Preheat a barbecue grill to medium and lightly grease with oil.

Cook the sausages, turning occasionally for about 10 minutes until cooked through.

HOMEMADE PORK & VEAL SAUSAGES

MAKES 2.5 KG

1.4 kg minced pork, at least 30% fat content (see note on page opposite), chilled
1 kg minced veal, chilled
½ cup finely chopped flat-leaf parsley
50 g (½ cup) powdered milk
50 g salt
3 teaspoons finely grated lemon zest
2 teaspoons ground white pepper
2 teaspoons ground mustard seeds
1 teaspoon ground celery seeds
1 teaspoon onion powder
natural pork sausage casings (see note on page opposite)

Place the pork and veal in a chilled mixing bowl and add the parsley, powdered milk, salt, lemon zest, white pepper, mustard seeds, celery and onion powder. Using your hands, mix well until the mixture becomes sticky. (This is an important step as it will improve the final texture.)

The flavouring can be checked at this stage by cooking a spoonful of pork mixture in a small frying pan with a little olive oil over medium–high heat. Taste and adjust the seasoning if necessary.

Run cold tap water through the sausage casing until the water runs clean. Cut a length of casing about 2 metres long and feed the casing onto the nozzle of a sausage maker. Leave a bit of casing hanging over to allow any excess air to escape. Feed the mince through the machine or nozzle, assisting the casing to slide off the nozzle as it is filled. Press out any air bubbles. Tie the end in a knot, and working towards the untied end, twist the filled casing into sausage lengths. Tie the open end in a knot. (If you don't have a sausage maker you can make the sausages by hand using a wide-necked funnel.)

Place the sausages onto a plate and cover with a clean dish towel. Refrigerate overnight or up to 48 hours before cooking (this allows the flavours to develop and also reduces the likelihood of the skins splitting).

Preheat a barbecue grill to medium and lightly grease with oil.

Cook the sausages, turning occasionally for about 10 minutes until cooked through.

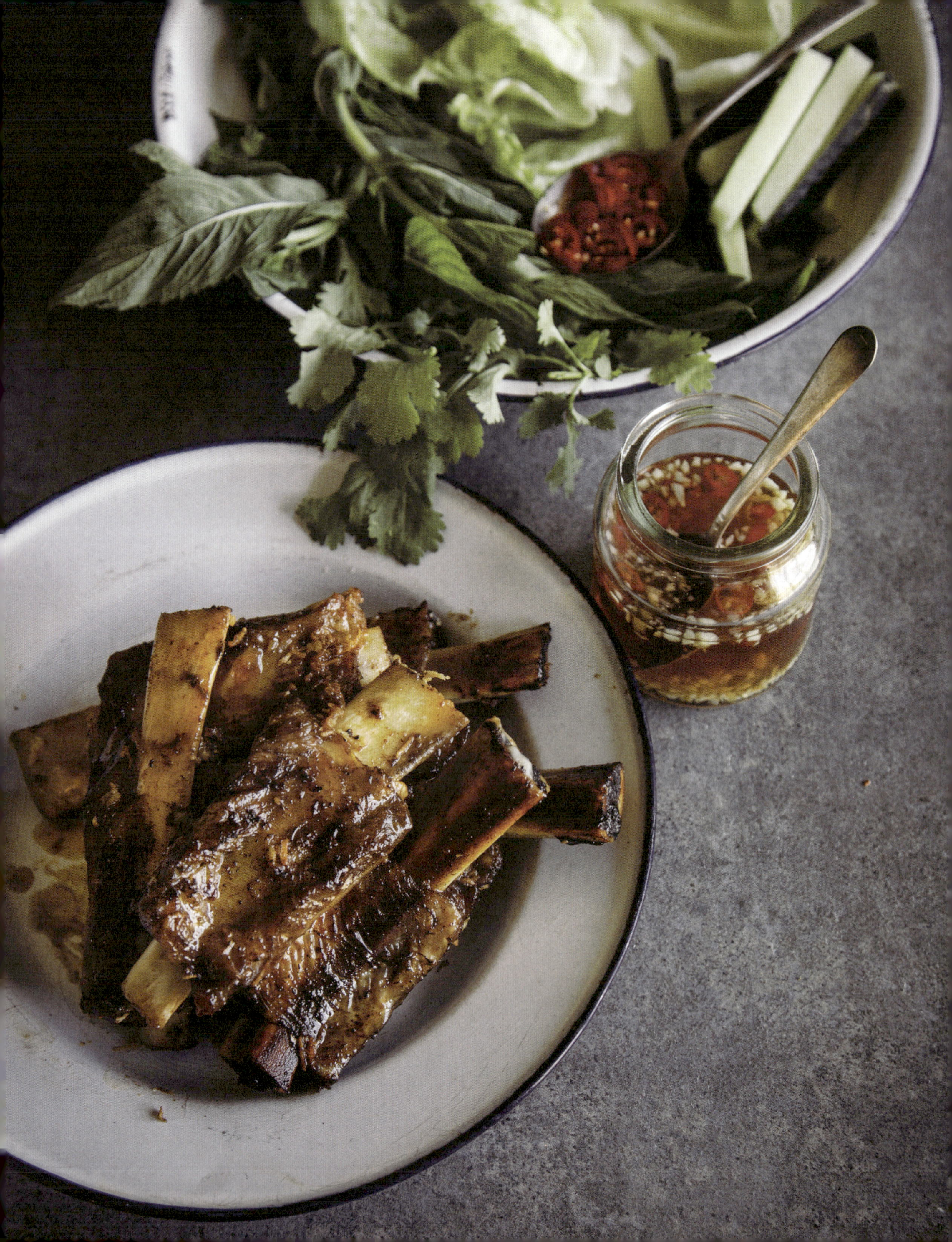

Grilled Pork Ribs with Vietnamese Dipping Sauce

SERVES 4

1.5 kg pork spare or baby back rib racks, cut into individual ribs
iceberg lettuce leaves, to serve
fresh mint sprigs, to serve
coriander sprigs, to serve
cucumber cut into sticks, to serve
small red chillies, sliced, to serve

MARINADE

4 French shallots, sliced
4 spring onions, roughly chopped
1 lemongrass stalk, white part only, chopped
1 cup coarsely chopped coriander stems, roots and leaves
5 cm piece ginger, peeled and sliced
6 garlic cloves, peeled
80 ml (⅓ cup) fish sauce
2 tablespoons soy sauce
1 tablespoon rice vinegar
2 tablespoons palm sugar
1 teaspoon ground white pepper

DIPPING SAUCE

60 ml (¼ cup) fish sauce
2 tablespoons rice vinegar
2 tablespoons caster sugar
2 garlic cloves, finely chopped
1 small red chilli, finely sliced
2 tablespoons lime juice

To make the marinade, place the ingredients in a food processor and process until finely chopped.

Place the pork ribs in a large bowl and coat well with the marinade. Cover with plastic wrap and refrigerate for up to 5 hours, tossing occasionally.

Preheat a hooded barbecue grill to medium–low and lightly grease with oil.

Place the ribs bone-side down on the grill, reserving the marinade for basting. Cover and cook, basting with the marinade every 15 minutes, for 1 hour. Turn the ribs, baste and reduce heat to low. Cover and cook for a further 30 minutes until tender.

Meanwhile, to make the dipping sauce, combine the fish sauce, vinegar and sugar with 80 ml (⅓ cup) water in a small saucepan over medium heat. Bring to just below boiling point then set aside to cool. Add the garlic, chilli and lime juice, and stir to combine.

Transfer the ribs to a serving platter and arrange the lettuce, mint, coriander, cucumber and chilli around them. Serve the dipping sauce in small bowls.

HOMEMADE BRATWURST

MAKES 3.5 KG

2.5 kg minced pork, at least 30% fat content (see note page 46), chilled
1 kg minced veal, chilled
70 g salt
1 tablespoon marjoram
1½ teaspoons ground white pepper
1 teaspoon mustard powder
1 teaspoon ground allspice
1 teaspoon onion powder
¼ teaspoon ground ginger
natural pork sausage casings (see note page 46)
crusty white rolls, to serve
seeded mustard, to serve

Place the pork and veal in a chilled mixing bowl and add the salt, marjoram, white pepper, mustard powder, allspice, onion powder and ginger. Using your hands, mix well until the mixture becomes sticky. (This is an important step as it will improve the final texture.)

The flavouring can be checked at this stage by cooking a spoonful of pork mixture in a small frying pan with a little olive oil over medium–high heat. Taste and adjust the seasoning if necessary.

Run cold tap water through the sausage casing until the water runs clean. Cut a length of casing about 2 metres long and feed the casing onto the nozzle of a sausage maker. Leave a bit of casing hanging over to allow any excess air to escape. Feed the mince through the machine or nozzle, assisting the casing to slide off the nozzle as it is filled. Press out any air bubbles. Tie the end in a knot, and working towards the untied end, twist the filled casing into sausage lengths. Tie the open end in a knot. (If you don't have a sausage maker you can make the sausages by hand using a wide-necked funnel.)

Place the sausages onto a plate and cover with a clean dish towel. Refrigerate overnight or up to 48 hours before cooking (this allows the flavours to develop and also reduces the likelihood of the skins splitting).

Preheat a barbecue grill to medium and lightly grease with oil.

Cook the sausages, turning occasionally for about 10 minutes until cooked through.

Serve in crusty white rolls spread with seeded mustard.

CURRYWURST
SERVES 4

4 Bratwurst sausages (see recipe on page opposite)

CURRY SAUCE
1 tablespoon vegetable oil
1 small white onion, finely chopped
1 garlic clove, crushed
1 tablespoon mild curry powder
600 ml tomato purée
80 ml (⅓ cup) white wine vinegar
75 g (⅓ cup) sugar
2 teaspoons worcestershire sauce
2 teaspoons salt
2 teaspoons sweet paprika
1 teaspoon mustard powder

To make the curry sauce, heat the oil in a saucepan over medium–low heat and add the onion. Cook for 3–4 minutes until soft and translucent. Add the garlic and cook for a further 2 minutes, making sure the garlic doesn't burn. Add the curry powder and cook, stirring, for 1 minute before adding the tomato purée. Heat until simmering, then add the vinegar, sugar, worcestershire sauce, salt, paprika and mustard powder. Simmer, uncovered, for 15 minutes or until thickened. Remove from the heat and process with a hand-held blender until smooth.

Preheat a barbecue grill to high and lightly grease with oil.

Score each sausage to one-quarter of its depth with a sharp knife at 1.5 cm intervals, to indicate bite-sized pieces. Cook the sausages for about 20 minutes until cooked through.

To serve, slice the sausages through the score lines. Transfer to serving plates and spoon the sauce over the top.

SOUTHERN-STYLE BABY BACK PORK RIBS

SERVES 4

1.5 kg pork baby back ribs, cut into racks of 4 ribs each
Grilled cabbage salad (page 164), to serve (optional)

DRY RUB

2 tablespoons sea salt flakes
1½ tablespoons sweet paprika
2 teaspoons smoked paprika
2 teaspoons garlic powder
1 teaspoon dried oregano
1 teaspoon celery salt
1 teaspoon chilli flakes

BARBECUE SAUCE

½ red onion, finely chopped
2 garlic cloves, finely chopped
2 tablespoons soft brown sugar
1 teaspoon sweet paprika
½ teaspoon smoked paprika
125 ml (½ cup) tomato ketchup
60 ml (¼ cup) cider vinegar
60 ml (¼ cup) pure maple syrup

Preheat a hooded barbecue grill to low heat.

To make the dry rub, combine the ingredients in a small bowl.

Coat the ribs in the dry rub, then wrap in foil. Place 2–3 racks in each foil package for easy handling.

Place the foil packs onto the grill and cover. Cook for 2 hours, turning every 30 minutes.

Meanwhile, to make the barbecue sauce, combine the ingredients in a small saucepan with 250 ml (1 cup) water. Cook over low heat for 20–25 minutes until thick. Reserve half the sauce for serving.

Remove the foil packages from the grill. Increase the heat to medium and lightly grease with oil. Carefully unwrap the ribs and discard the foil. Brush the ribs all over with the remaining barbecue sauce and return to the grill. Cook, basting and turning regularly, for 30 minutes, until the ribs are browned and sticky, caramelised and charred.

Pile the ribs onto a serving platter and serve with the reserved barbecue sauce and, if desired, Grilled cabbage salad.

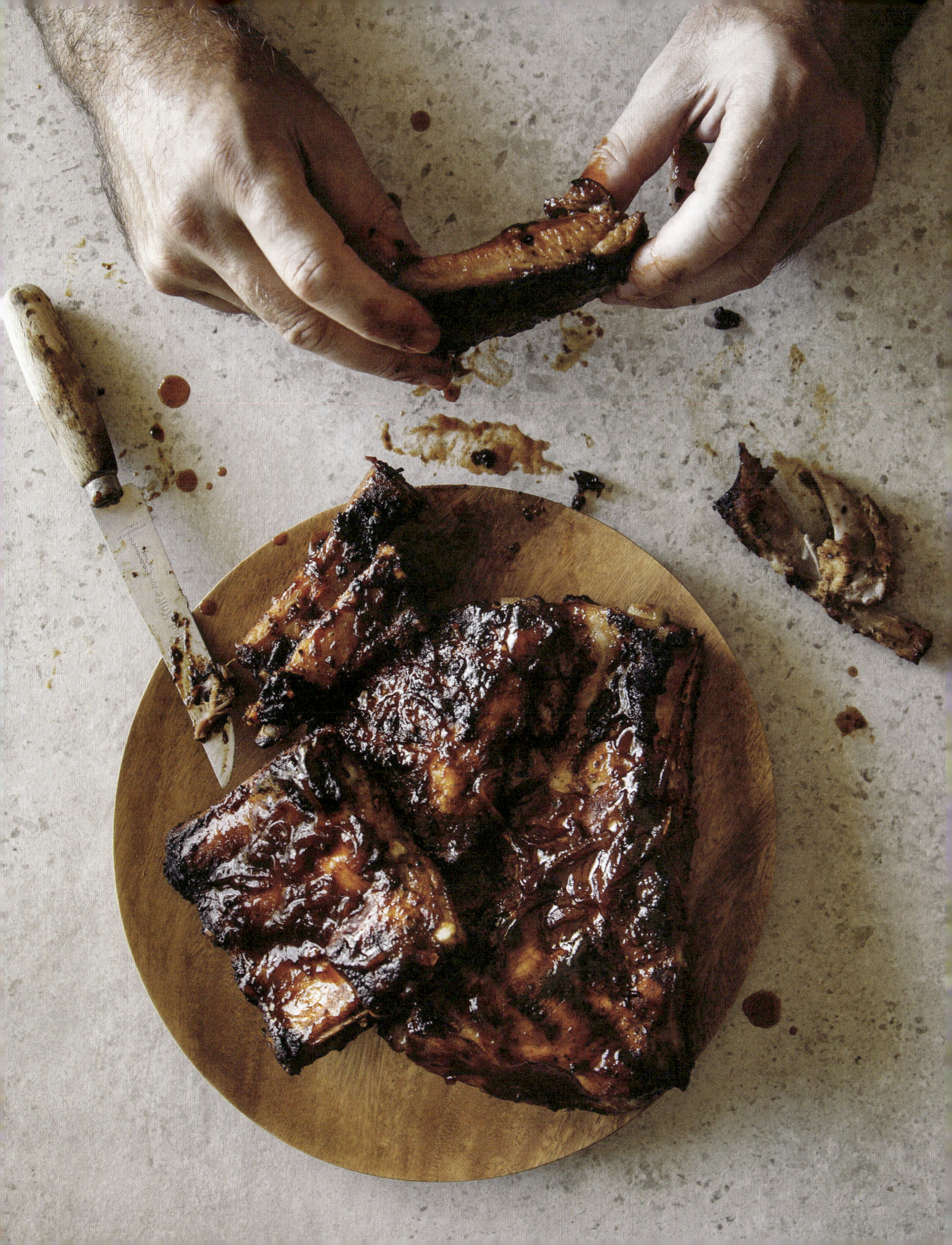

BACON-WEAVE CHEESEBURGERS SERVES 4

600 g minced beef
2 onions: 1 grated; 1 thinly sliced
1 teaspoon dijon mustard
1 large egg, beaten
40 g (½ cup) fresh breadcrumbs
35 g (⅓ cup) finely grated parmesan cheese
12 slices rindless streaky bacon
4 soft burger buns, split horizontally
4 slices Swiss cheese
1 red onion, thinly sliced
mayonnaise, sliced dill pickles, shredded lettuce and thinly sliced tomato, to serve

Preheat the oven to 180°C. Line a baking tray with foil, folding up the edges of the foil to contain the rendered bacon fat.

Combine the beef, grated onion, mustard, egg, breadcrumbs and parmesan in a bowl. Season, mix with damp hands, and then form into four patties. Chill for 30 minutes.

Meanwhile, make a weave or lattice with the bacon strips to form a square on the prepared tray. Place an upturned wire rack over the bacon to keep it flat while it cooks. Cook the bacon for 25–30 minutes until browned and crisp. Remove from the oven, carefully remove the rack and place the bacon weave on paper towel. Cut into four even squares. Reserve the rendered fat from the bacon tray. Turn off the oven, place the bacon weave on the tray and return to the oven to keep warm.

Preheat a barbecue hotplate to high and lightly grease with oil.

Brush the cut side of each of the buns with the reserved bacon fat. Set aside.

Place the patties on the hotplate, flatten slightly and cook for 8–10 minutes until well crusted and browned, turning occasionally. Top the patties with the cheese slices and cook for a minute or so more until the cheese starts to melt and the patties are just cooked through. Transfer to a plate.

Meanwhile, add the sliced onion to the hotplate and cook, stirring often, for 4–5 minutes until tender and browned. Pile on top of the cheese on the patties.

Grill the cut side of the burger buns until golden. Spread mayonnaise on the toasted side of each bun. Place a few slices of pickle on each bottom bun. Top with lettuce, tomato, a patty and a square of bacon weave. Close the buns and serve immediately.

BACONWRAPPED MAC & CHEESEBURGERS MAKES 6

250 g macaroni
40 g butter
2 shallots, finely chopped
1½ tablespoons plain flour, plus extra for coating
250 ml (1 cup) full-cream milk
125 g (1 cup) grated gruyère or smoked cheddar cheese
75 g (¾ cup) finely grated parmesan cheese
2 large eggs, lightly beaten
80 g (1⅓ cups) panko (Japanese) breadcrumbs
125 ml (½ cup) sunflower or vegetable oil
6 slices middle bacon, rind removed
6 rolls or brioche buns, halved and toasted
dijonnaise, good quality aioli or smoky tomato ketchup, to serve

Line a 33 cm x 23 cm baking tray with baking paper. Bring a large saucepan of salted water to the boil. Cook the macaroni according to the packet directions or until al dente, stirring often to prevent sticking. Drain.

Meanwhile, melt the butter in a saucepan. Add the shallots and cook for 3–4 minutes until soft. Stir in the flour. Remove from the heat and slowly stir in the milk. Return to the heat and gently bring to the boil, stirring until thickened. Remove from the heat and stir in the cheeses until melted. Season with salt and pepper then stir in the macaroni until well combined. Pour into the prepared tray, pressing down with a wooden spoon to compact the macaroni mixture. Refrigerate for at least 3 hours to set.

Preheat a barbecue grill to high and lightly grease with oil.

Turn the macaroni out onto a clean work surface and cut into six rounds using a 9 cm cutter. (Save any leftover mac and cheese and reheat as a snack.)

Place the extra flour, egg and breadcrumbs into three separate shallow bowls. Coat each macaroni patty in the flour, shaking off the excess, followed by the beaten egg, then into the breadcrumbs, pressing on to coat well. Place onto a plate.

Heat the oil in a large non-stick frying pan until very hot. Shallow-fry the patties, three at a time, for 2–3 minutes on each side until golden. Transfer to a plate lined with paper towel to drain.

Wrap a rasher of bacon the whole way around each patty and secure the ends with a toothpick. Butter the cut sides of the buns. Cook the bacon-wrapped patties on the grill for 3–4 minutes on each side, or until the bacon is golden. Remove the toothpicks. Grill the cut sides of the buns.

Serve the patties on the toasted buns spread with dijonnaise, topped with lettuce and tomato.

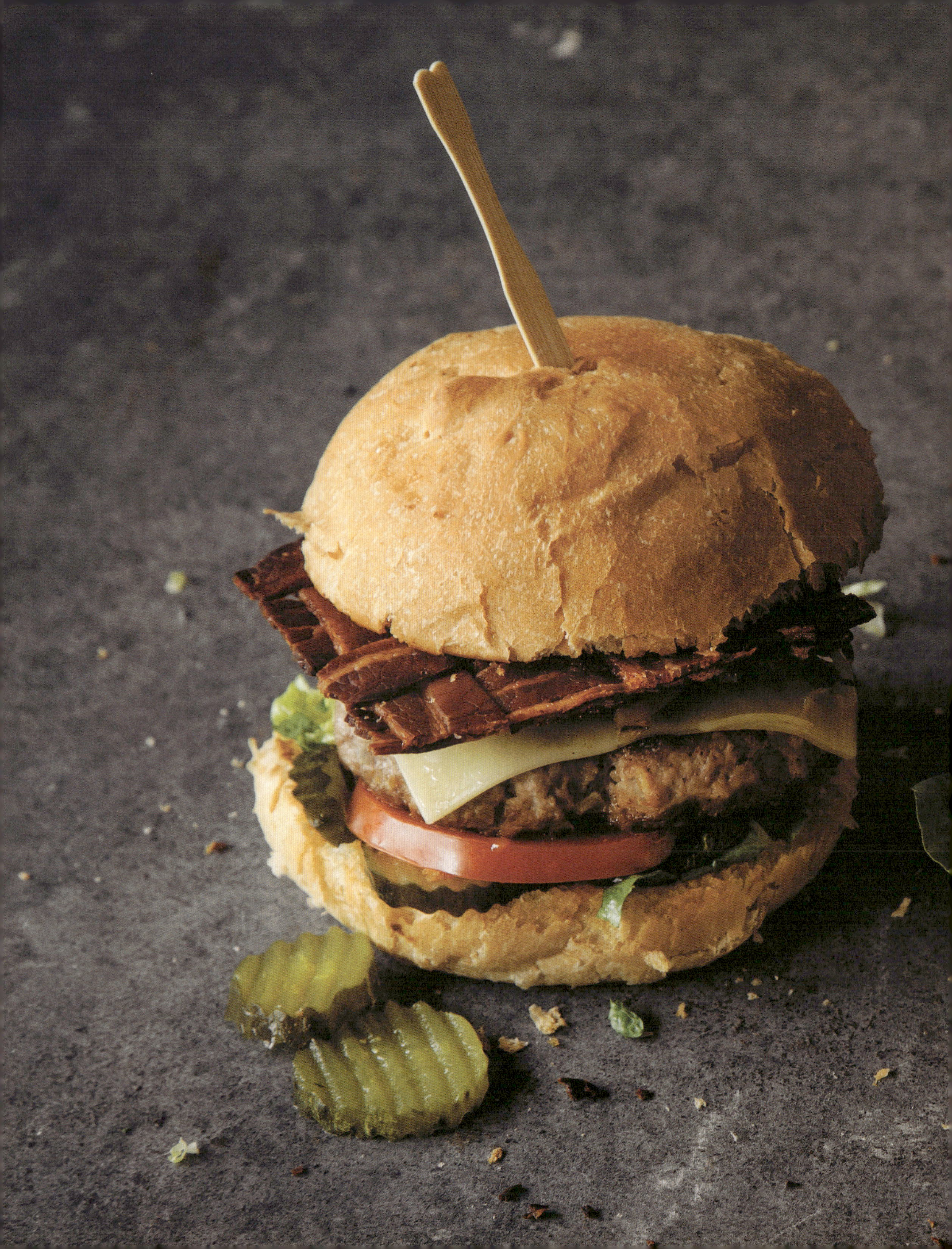

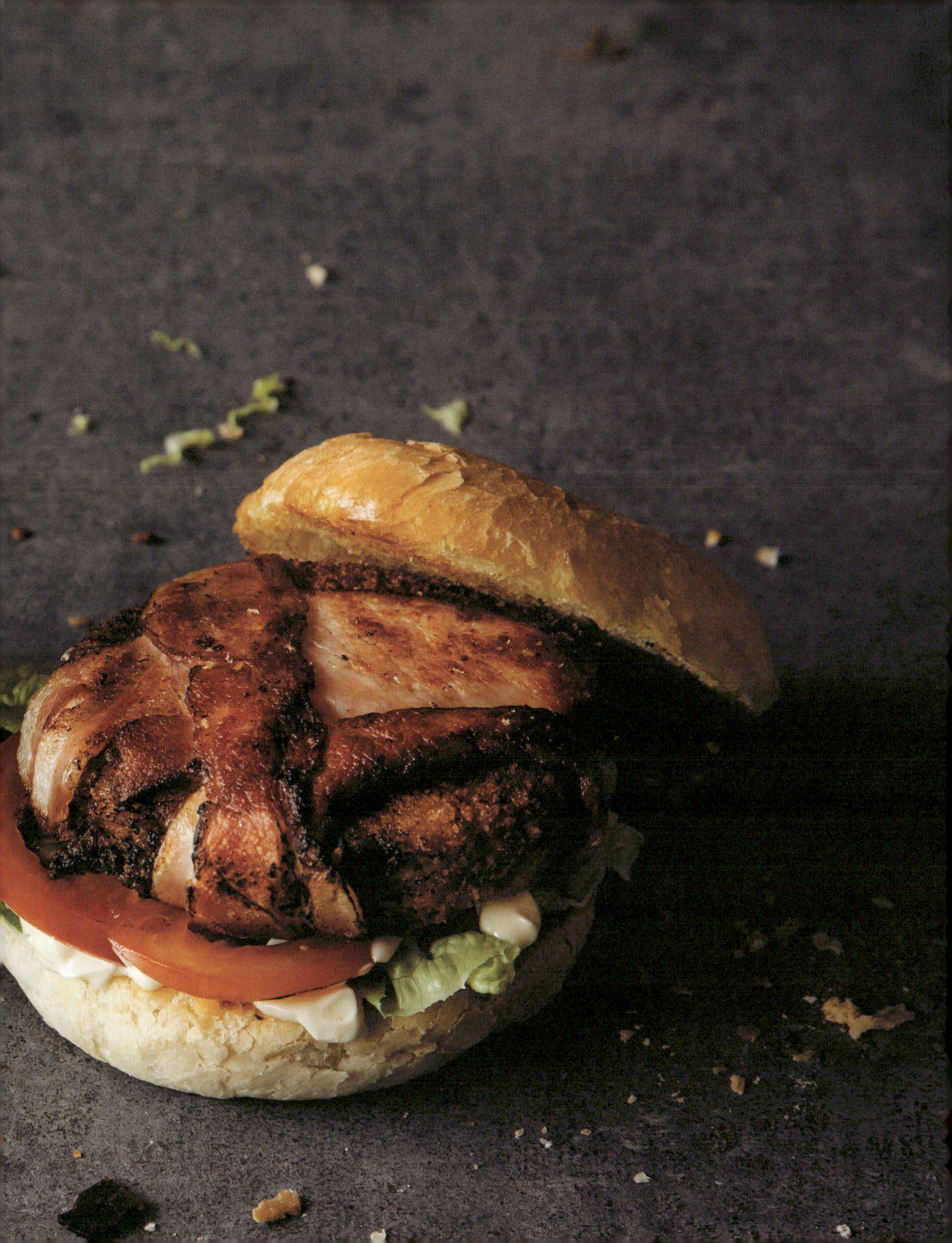

SMOKEY CHIPOTLE BARBECUED PORK RIBS

SERVES 4

4 racks pork baby back ribs, each cut in half

DRY RUB

3 teaspoons sea salt flakes
3 teaspoons smoked paprika
2 teaspoons soft brown sugar
2 teaspoons dried oregano
1½ teaspoons freshly ground black pepper

SAUCE

1 tablespoon olive oil
2 garlic cloves, crushed
2 cooking apples, peeled, cored and grated
1 teaspoon sea salt
1 teaspoon sweet paprika
2 chipotle chillies in adobo sauce, chopped
250 ml (1 cup) tomato passata
60 ml (¼ cup) maple syrup
2 tablespoons cider vinegar

Preheat the oven to 150°C.

Combine the dry rub ingredients in a small bowl. Sprinkle evenly over both sides of the pork ribs, pressing it in well. Wrap the ribs in foil, then place in a single layer on a large baking tray. Transfer to the oven and bake for 2½ hours. Remove the foil-wrapped ribs from the oven and leave until cool enough to handle.

To make the sauce, heat the olive oil in a small saucepan over low heat and cook the garlic and apple for about 4 minutes, or until soft. Stir in the salt, paprika, chillies, passata, maple syrup and vinegar. Continue to cook over low heat, stirring occasionally, for about 10 minutes, or until the mixture is thick and saucy. Set aside.

Preheat a barbecue grill to medium heat.

Unwrap the ribs, and brush the sauce over both sides. Grill the ribs on both sides, until charred. Transfer the ribs to a chopping board. Use a sharp knife to cut between the bones.

Pile the ribs onto a platter to serve.

JAMAICAN JERK PORK BELLY

SERVES 8

1.5 kg pork belly
Apple & cabbage slaw (page 144),
  to serve (optional)

JERK MARINADE

6 spring onions, roughly chopped
2 garlic cloves, roughly chopped
3 scotch bonnet chillies, deseeded
  (if you prefer less heat) and sliced
2 cm piece ginger, peeled and grated
2 tablespoons soft brown sugar
2 tablespoons fresh thyme leaves
2 tablespoons ground allspice
1 tablespoon sea salt flakes
2 teaspoons nutmeg
2 teaspoons ground cinnamon
2 bay leaves, torn
125 ml (½ cup) olive oil
60 ml (¼ cup) soy sauce
juice of 1 lime
zest and juice of 1 orange
125 ml (½ cup) cider vinegar

To make the marinade, place the ingredients in a food processor and blend until smooth.

Place the pork in a baking dish. Pour the marinade over and massage into the pork. Cover with plastic wrap and refrigerate for at least 2 hours, or overnight.

Preheat a barbecue grill to medium–high and lightly grease with oil.

Place the pork on the grill, reserving the excess marinade for basting. Cook for 10–15 minutes on each side, then reduce the heat to low. Continue to cook, basting and turning every 20 minutes for 1½ hours, or until dark and tender.

Remove from heat, cover and rest for 15 minutes before slicing.

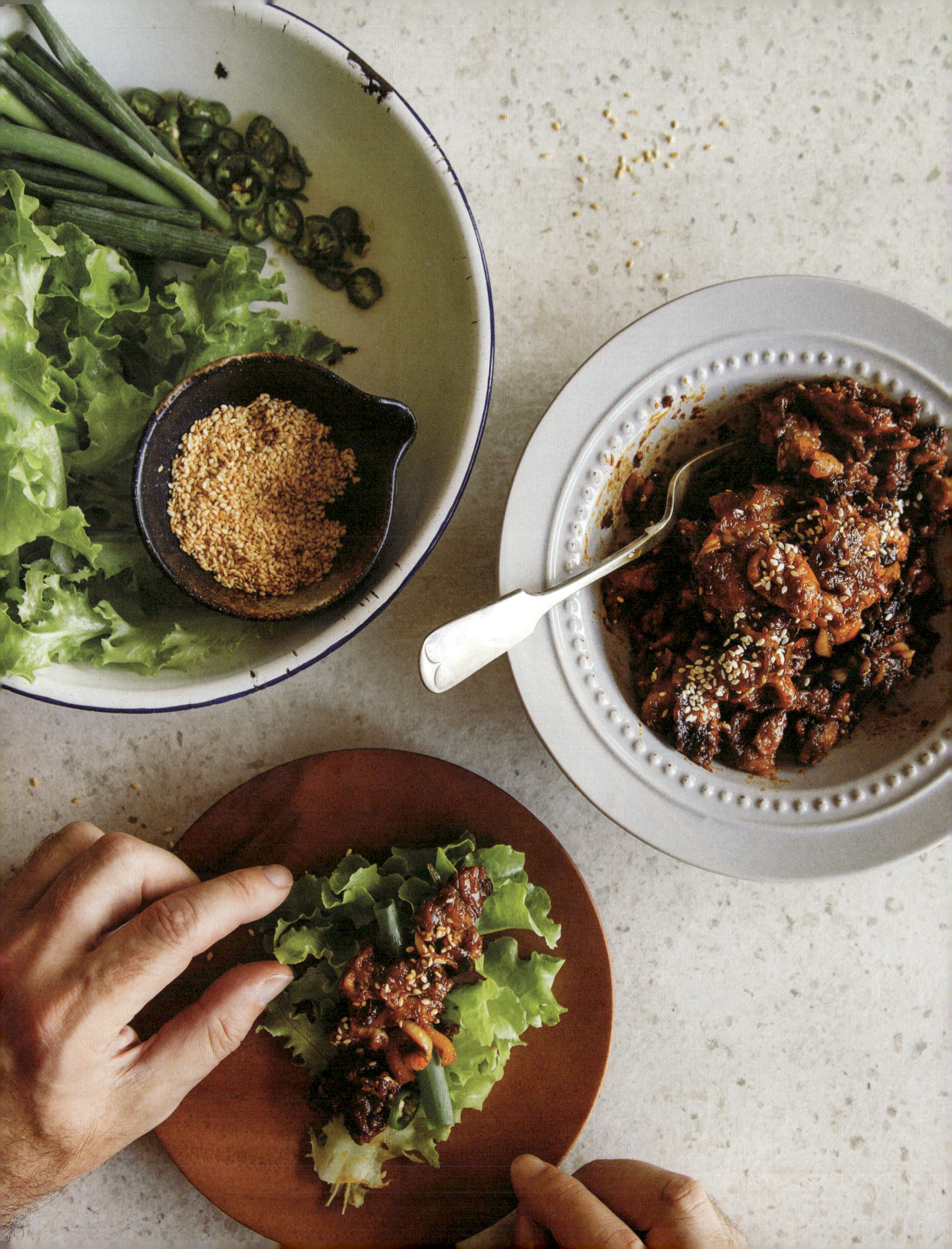

KOREAN BARBECUED PORK

SERVES 6

1 kg pork belly, cut into 8 cm pieces, then very thinly sliced
oakleaf lettuce leaves, to serve
spring onions cut into 10 cm lengths, to serve
sliced green chillies, to serve
toasted sesame seeds, to serve

MARINADE

½ onion, sliced
½ cup grated nashi pear
3 spring onions, finely chopped
4 garlic cloves, crushed
½ teaspoon grated ginger
3 tablespoons gochujang (Korean red pepper paste)
45 g (¼ cup) soft brown sugar
2 tablespoons rice cooking wine
1 tablespoon soy sauce
2 teaspoons sesame oil
1 tablespoon sesame seeds
2 tablespoons fish sauce

To make the marinade, combine the ingredients in a large bowl. Season with pepper. Add the pork and mix to coat well. Cover with plastic wrap and refrigerate for at least 2 hours.

Heat a barbecue hotplate to high and lightly grease with oil.

Cook the pork in batches. Place pieces of pork on the hotplate in a single layer (avoid crowding). Cook for 2 minutes on each side or until caramelised. Transfer to a serving plate and keep warm while the remaining pork is cooked.

Arrange the lettuce leaves, spring onions, chillies on the serving plate around the pork. Sprinkle with the sesame seeds and serve.

SEAFOOD

SPICED FISH TACOS WITH CHIPOTLE SAUCE
page 64

LOUISIANA PRAWN PO'BOY
page 67

WHOLE SNAPPER WITH THAI FLAVOURS
page 68

GRILLED TUNA WITH GARLIC & CAPER AIOLI
page 69

FLOUNDER WITH BURNT BUTTER, CAPERS & SAGE
page 70

JAPANESE SEVEN-SPICE CALAMARI
page 73

SUGARCANE PRAWNS
page 74

PROSCIUTTO-WRAPPED SCALLOPS
page 75

LOBSTER TAIL & SALAD SLIDERS
page 76

CRISPY SKIN SALMON WITH FENNEL & CELERY REMOULADE
page 79

SPICED FISH TACOS WITH CHIPOTLE SAUCE

SERVES 4–6

1 kg firm white fish (such as snapper or ling), cut into 10 cm x 3 cm pieces
olive oil, for brushing
2 cups coriander leaves, roughly chopped
1 white onion, very finely chopped
¼ green cabbage, finely shredded
6 radishes, thinly shaved
12 corn tortillas
3 limes, cut into wedges

CHIPOTLE SAUCE

125 g (½ cup) whole egg mayonnaise
125 g (½ cup) Greek-style yoghurt
1 small chipotle chilli in adobo sauce, finely chopped, plus 1 teaspoon of sauce
½ teaspoon dried oregano
1 tablespoon finely chopped dill
zest and juice of 1 lime

SPICE MIX

1 teaspoon paprika
½ teaspoon ground cumin
½ teaspoon freshly ground black pepper
½ teaspoon dried oregano
½ teaspoon sea salt flakes

To make the sauce, place the ingredients in a blender and blend until smooth. Transfer to a serving bowl and season to taste. Cover with plastic wrap and refrigerate until needed.

Preheat a barbecue hotplate to medium–high and lightly grease with oil.

To make the spice mix, combine the ingredients in a small bowl.

Pat the fish dry with paper towel, then brush with olive oil and sprinkle with the spice mix. Cover with plastic wrap and refrigerate for 10 minutes.

Combine the coriander and onion in a small bowl.

Cook the fish, turning once, for approximately 2 minutes each side or until just cooked through.

Toast the tortillas on one side on the hotplate or grill for about 30 seconds or until lightly charred.

Serve the fish in a pile along with the tortillas, chipotle sauce, coriander and onion, a pile of the cabbage and radishes, and lime wedges.

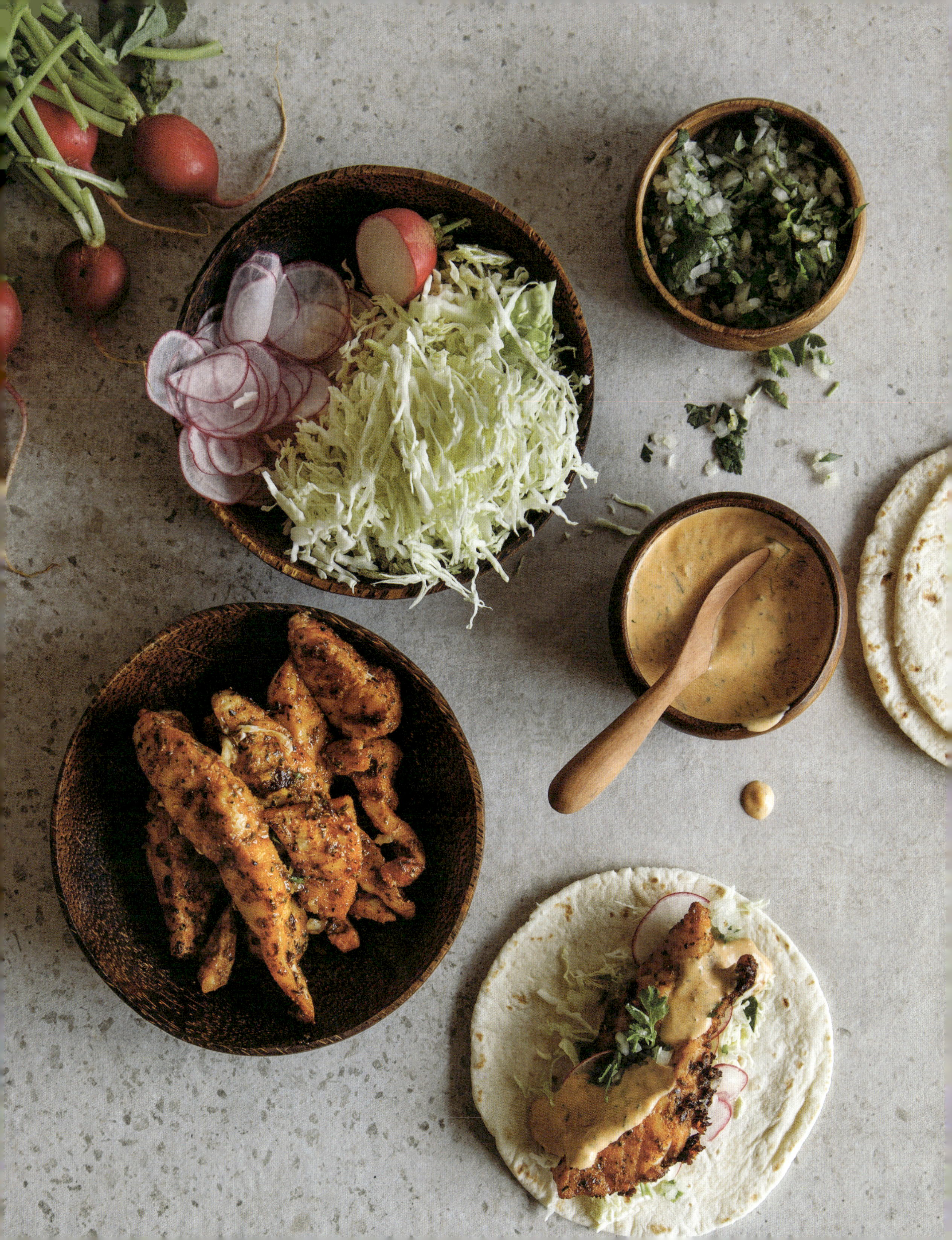

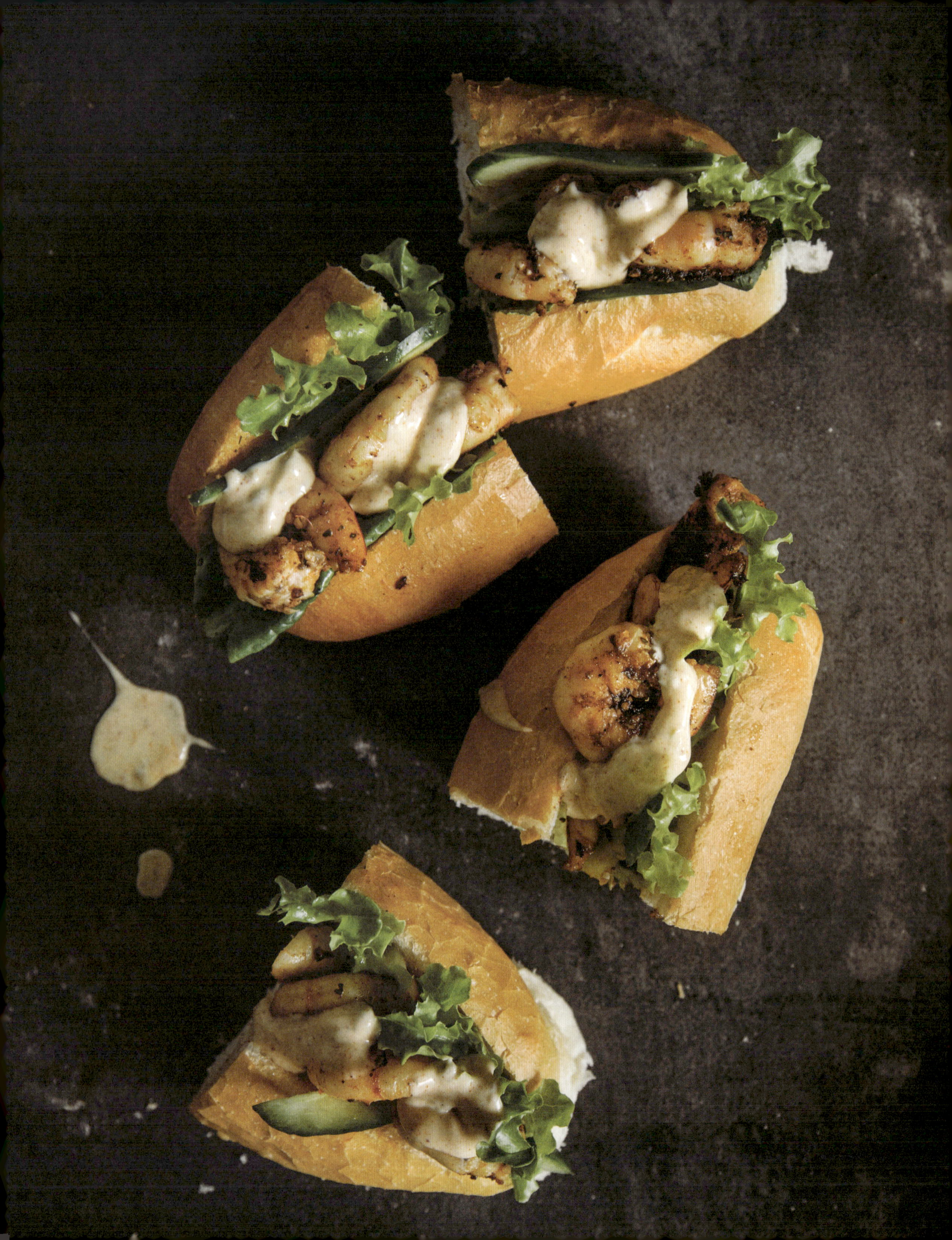

LOUISIANA PRAWN PO'BOY

SERVES 4

600 g large raw prawns, shelled and deveined

bamboo skewers, soaked in cold water

1 long baguette, cut into 4 lengths then halved

2 cucumbers, sliced into thin lengths

½ green oakleaf lettuce, washed and drained thoroughly

LOUISIANA MARINADE

2 tablespoons olive oil

1 garlic clove, finely chopped

1 teaspoon sweet paprika

½ teaspoon salt

¼ teaspoon freshly ground black pepper

¼ teaspoon cayenne pepper

½ teaspoon dried oregano

½ teaspoon dried thyme

REMOULADE

125 g (½ cup) good-quality whole egg mayonnaise

1 teaspoon dijon mustard

juice of ½ lemon

2 teaspoons capers, roughly chopped

¼ teaspoon cayenne pepper

¼ teaspoon sweet paprika

To make the marinade, combine the ingredients in a large mixing bowl. Add the prawns and toss to coat well. Cover and refrigerate for 30 minutes.

To make the remoulade, combine the ingredients in a small mixing bowl. Mix well and set aside.

Heat the barbecue grill to medium and lightly grease with oil.

Thread the prawns onto the bamboo skewers and cook for 2–3 minutes on each side.

Fill the baguettes with cucumber and lettuce. Remove the prawns from the skewers and pile onto the lettuce. Top with remoulade and serve.

WHOLE SNAPPER WITH THAI FLAVOURS SERVES 4

3 long red chillies, deseeded and coarsely chopped
2 lemongrass stalks, white part only, thinly sliced
1 tablespoon grated palm sugar
½ bunch coriander, leaves picked and stems roughly chopped
1 tablespoon fish sauce
2 tablespoons coconut milk
1 kg whole snapper, cleaned and scaled
2 limes, sliced, plus extra lime wedges to serve
4 kaffir lime leaves, torn
banana leaves, for wrapping

Preheat a barbecue grill to medium-high and lightly grease with oil.

Pound the chillies, lemongrass, palm sugar and coriander to a coarse paste using a mortar and pestle. Transfer to a small mixing bowl, add the fish sauce and coconut milk and stir to combine.

Lay the banana leaves out on a large board, overlapping to form a piece large enough to wrap the fish.

Make four diagonal, 1 cm deep cuts in each side of the snapper. Coat the top of the fish with half the chilli paste, working it into the cuts. Place the fish, paste-side down, in the centre of the banana leaves. Fill the cavity with lime slices and kaffir lime leaves and spread the chilli paste over the fish. Wrap the banana leaves to enclose, then wrap in foil.

Place the parcel on the grill and cook for 8 minutes on each side, until just cooked through.

Serve with lime wedges.

GRILLED TUNA WITH GARLIC & CAPER AIOLI

SERVES 4

4 tuna steaks, 2 cm thick
Summer veg ratatouille parcels (page 134), to serve (optional)

GARLIC & CAPER AIOLI
2 garlic cloves, crushed
1 teaspoon sea salt flakes
2 egg yolks
250 ml (1 cup) olive oil
1 tablespoon lemon juice
1½ tablespoons baby capers, drained
1 tablespoon finely chopped flat-leaf parsley

MARINADE
zest of 1 lemon, finely grated
1 tablespoon sea salt flakes
1 teaspoon coarse ground black pepper
60 ml (¼ cup) olive oil

To make the aioli, place the garlic, salt and egg yolks in a small food processor and blend until well combined. With the motor running, add the oil in a thin, steady stream, until the aioli thickens. Transfer to a small bowl. Stir in the lemon juice, capers and parsley. Cover and refrigerate until required.

To make the marinade, combine the ingredients in a small bowl. Brush the tuna with the marinade and place in a zip-lock bag and refrigerate for at least 2 hours, or overnight.

Preheat a barbecue grill to high and lightly grease with oil.

Allow the tuna to come to room temperature before cooking.

Cook the tuna steaks for about 2 minutes until the red tuna turns beige part of the way up the side. Turn and cook for another 2 minutes, until the colour of the tuna changes as before and you can just see a line of pink from the side.

Serve with a generous dollop of the aioli, and if you like, Summer veg ratatouille parcels to accompany.

FLOUNDER WITH BURNT BUTTER, CAPERS & SAGE

SERVES 4

4 x 500 g whole flounder, rinsed and dried
2 tablespoons olive oil
banana leaves, for wrapping
100 g butter
⅓ cup capers, drained
20 sage leaves
lemon cheeks, to serve

Brush each flounder with oil and season with salt.

Place a large sheet of foil onto a clean work surface. Cover with a banana leaf. Place one flounder on the banana leaf, top-side down, and wrap carefully to enclose.

Repeat with the remaining fish.

Preheat a barbecue hotplate to medium–high and lightly grease with oil.

Cook the flounder for 4–5 minutes, turn and continue cooking for 2–3 minutes until cooked through.

Meanwhile, place a small frying pan on the hotplate to heat. Add the butter and swirl in the pan to heat evenly. When it starts to foam, add the capers and sage and cook for 1 minute or until crisp.

Serve each flounder on its banana leaf and spoon the hot butter, capers and sage over the top, with a lemon cheek alongside.

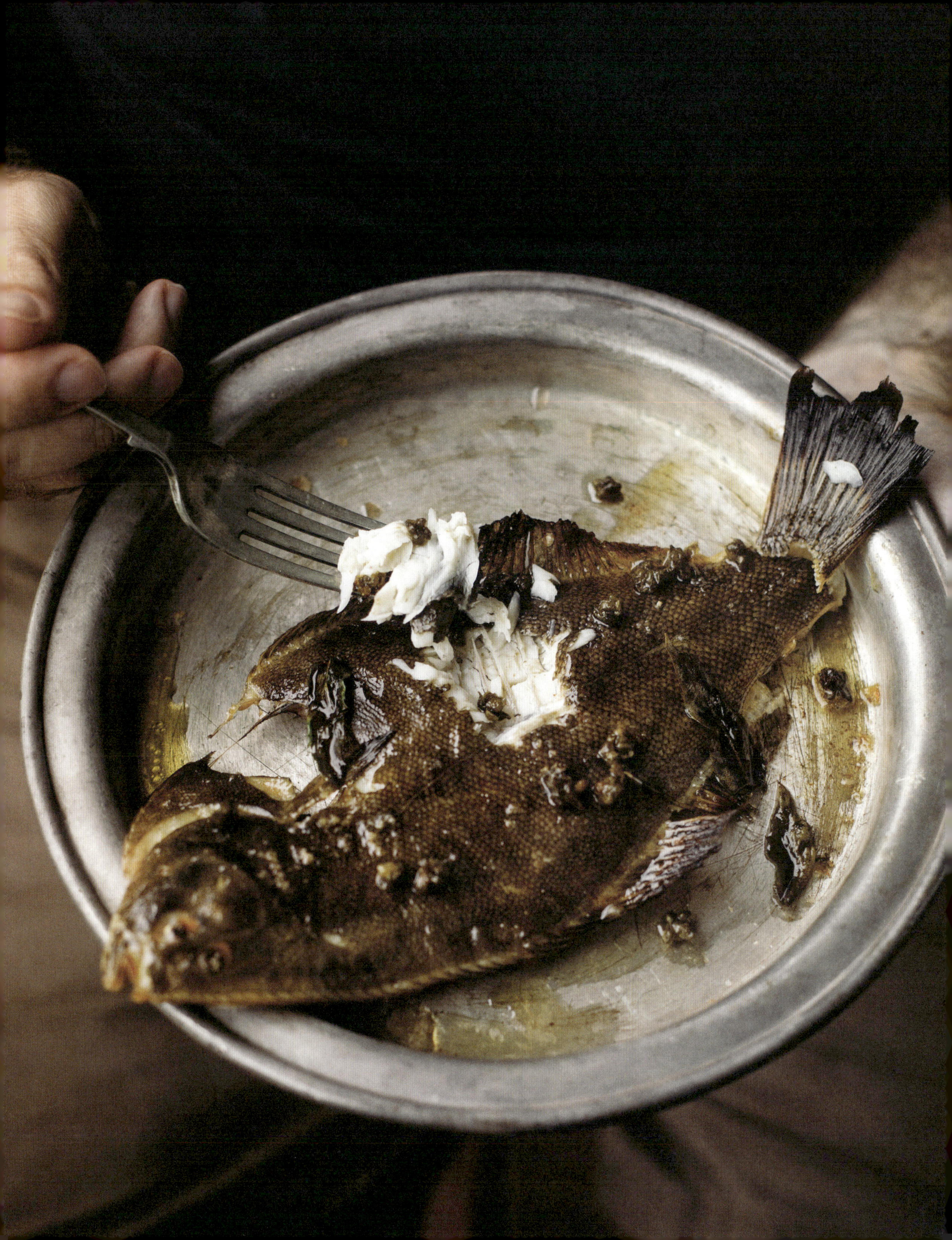

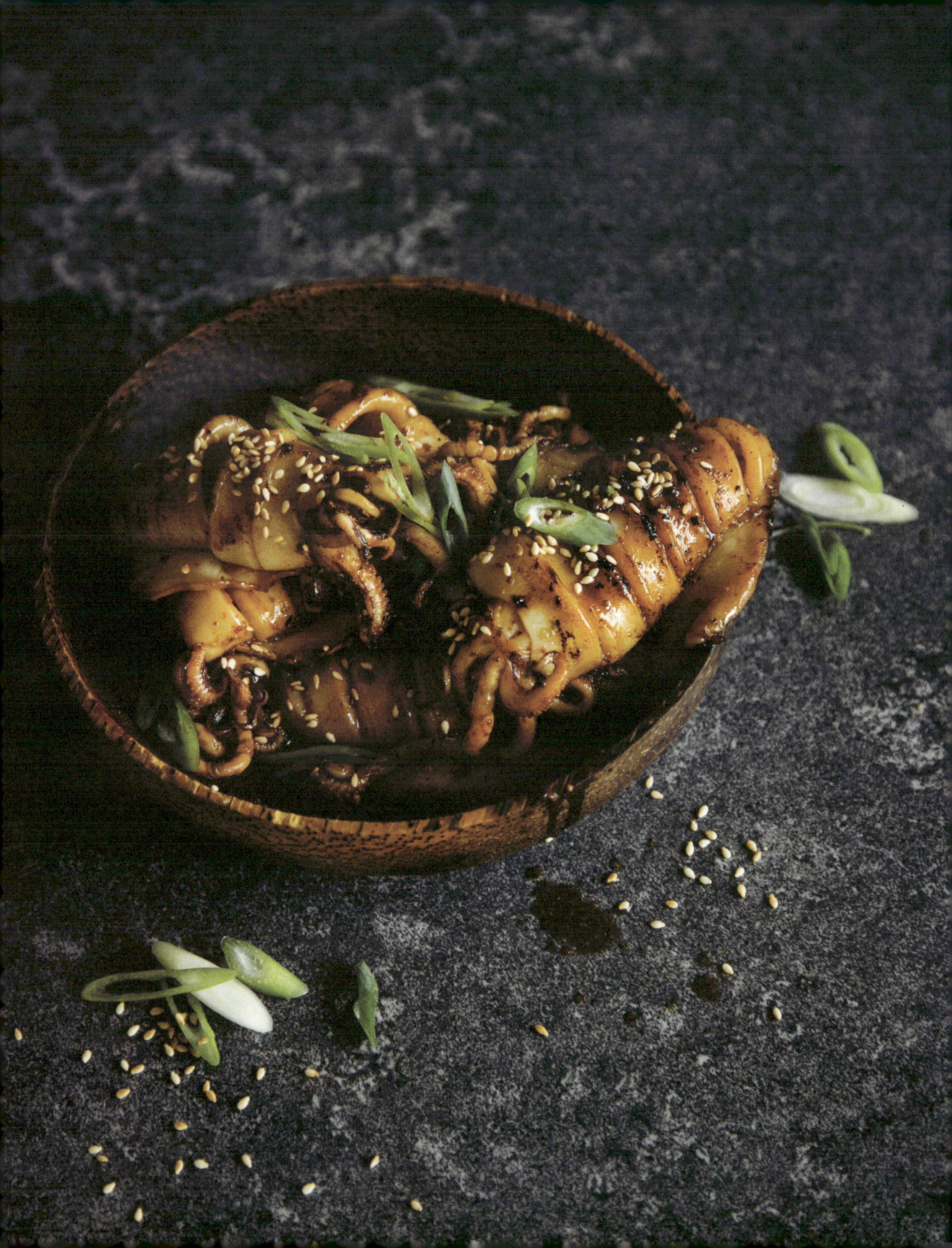

JAPANESE SEVEN-SPICE CALAMARI

SERVES 4

500 g squid hoods, cleaned and cut into 2 cm rings, leave tentacles intact
2 tablespoons sesame seeds, toasted until golden
2 spring onions, thinly sliced on the diagonal

JAPANESE MARINADE

125 ml (½ cup) light soy sauce
5 cm piece of ginger, peeled and finely grated (approximately 2 tablespoons)
3 tablespoons mirin
1 tablespoon shichimi togarashi (see note)
1 tablespoon peanut oil

To make the marinade, combine the ingredients in a large bowl. Reserve half the marinade for basting.

Add the squid to the remaining marinade and mix well to coat. Set aside in the refrigerator to marinate for 15 minutes.

Preheat a barbecue grill to high and lightly grease with oil.

Grill the squid, turning frequently and basting with reserved marinade, for 2–3 minutes until opaque and tender. Take care not to overcook the squid as it can quickly become rubbery.

Serve garnished with toasted sesame seeds and spring onions.

Note: Shichimi togarashi is a traditional Japanese seven-spice mix, predominately made up of red pepper, and is available from Asian supermarkets.

SUGARCANE PRAWNS

SERVES 4–6

8 garlic cloves, roughly chopped
5 Asian shallots, roughly chopped
4 lemongrass stalks, white part only, finely chopped
2 tablespoons grated palm sugar
2 tablespoons light fish sauce
1.5 kg raw prawns, shelled and deveined
1 egg white
1 tablespoon finely chopped coriander leaves
white pepper, to taste
4 pieces canned sugar cane, cut lengthways into 1 cm pieces

NUOC CHAM DIPPING SAUCE

2 tablespoons caster sugar
80 ml (⅓ cup) rice vinegar
80 ml (⅓ cup) fish sauce
60 ml (¼ cup) lime juice
2 garlic cloves, very finely chopped
1 long red chilli, finely sliced

Place the garlic, shallots, lemongrass and palm sugar in a food processor and pulse to a paste. Add the fish sauce, prawns and egg white and process until smooth. Stir in the coriander and white pepper.

With damp hands, form a portion of the prawn mixture around the end of a sugarcane piece, so that the mixture covers about two-thirds of the stick. Place on a lightly greased baking tray and repeat with the remaining prawn mixture and sugarcane pieces. Cover and refrigerate for 30 minutes.

Preheat a barbecue grill to high and lightly grease with oil.

Meanwhile, to make the nuoc cham, combine the sugar, vinegar, fish sauce and 125 ml water in a small saucepan over low–medium heat. Bring to a gentle simmer and stir until the sugar has dissolved. Remove from the heat and set aside to cool slightly. Mix in the lime juice, garlic and chilli. Set aside to cool to room temperature.

Cook the sugarcane prawns for about 5 minutes, turning occasionally, until golden all over. Serve hot with the dipping sauce alongside.

PROSCIUTTO-WRAPPED SCALLOPS SERVES 4

12 large scallops, cleaned
olive oil, for drizzling
juice of 1 lemon
2 sprigs thyme, leaves picked
salt and freshly ground black pepper
6 slices prosciutto, cut in half lengthways
4 bamboo skewers, soaked in cold water

Preheat a barbecue hotplate to high and lightly grease with oil.

Drizzle the scallops lightly with olive oil and sprinkle with the lemon juice and thyme. Season with salt and pepper.

Wrap each scallop carefully with a slice of prosciutto and thread onto the bamboo skewers.

Cook for 1½ minutes on each side and serve immediately.

LOBSTER TAIL & SALAD SLIDERS

MAKES 8 SLIDERS

2 tablespoons butter, softened
2 tablespoons finely chopped flat-leaf parsley
zest of 1 lemon
pinch of sea salt flakes
2 lobster tails, halved lengthways
1 celery stalk, finely sliced
½ red apple, finely sliced
1 tablespoon finely chopped dill
2 tablespoons whole egg mayonnaise
2 tablespoons crème fraîche
1 butter lettuce, leaves separated
8 slider buns, split and toasted

Preheat barbecue grill to high and lightly grease with oil.

Combine the butter, parsley, lemon zest and salt in a bowl.

Place the lobster tail halves, cut-side down, on the grill and cook for 2–3 minutes until slightly charred. Turn and spread lobster tails with the seasoned butter. Continue grilling for a further 3–5 minutes until the lobster meat is tender. Remove from the heat, cover loosely and set aside to cool.

Toss the celery, apple and dill together a bowl. Add the mayonnaise and crème fraîche and mix well.

Remove the lobster meat from the shells and chop into 1 cm discs. Stir gently into the salad, coating well with the dressing.

Place the lettuce leaves onto the bun bases, and divide the salad equally between the 8 buns. Top with the lids and secure with toothpicks. Serve immediately.

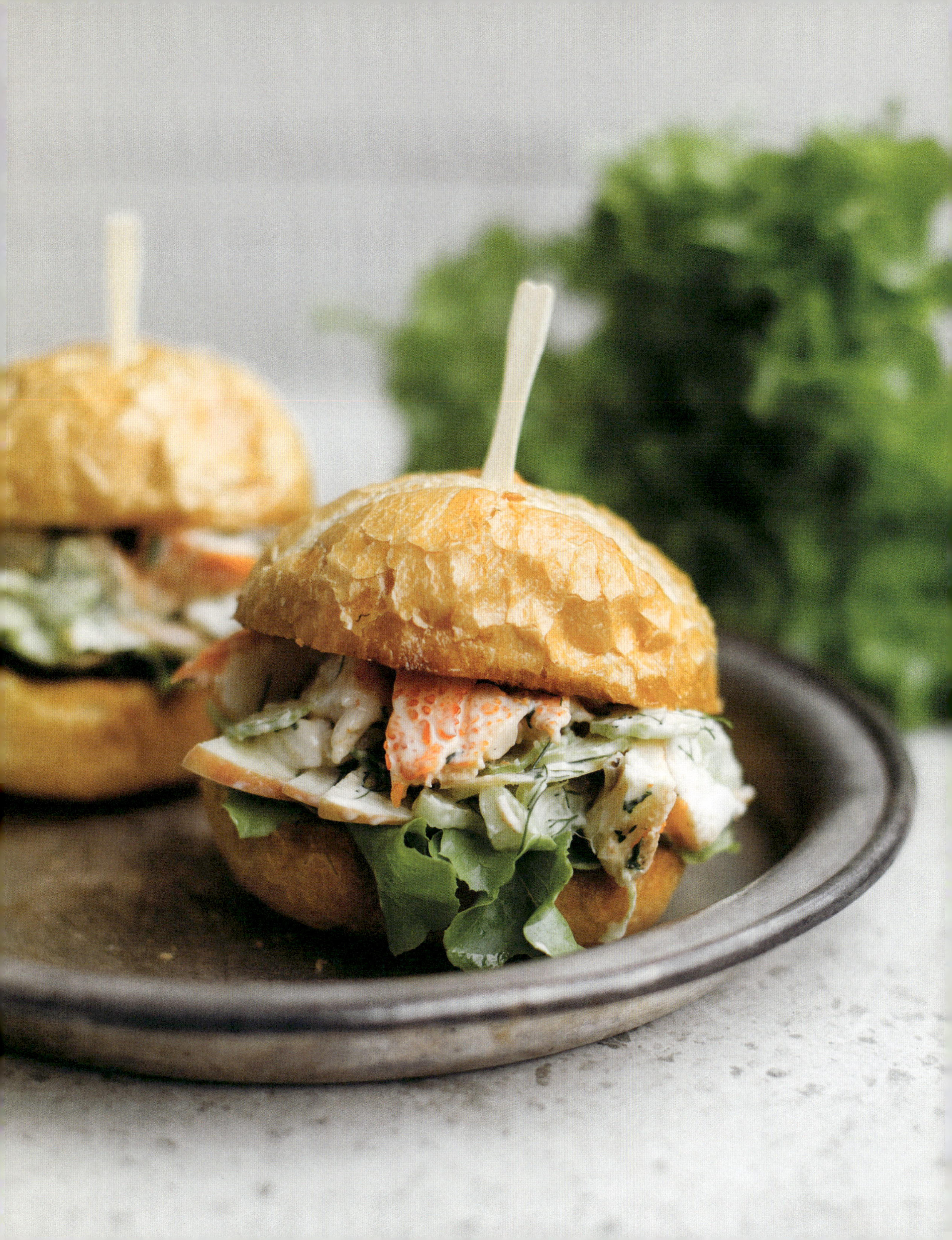

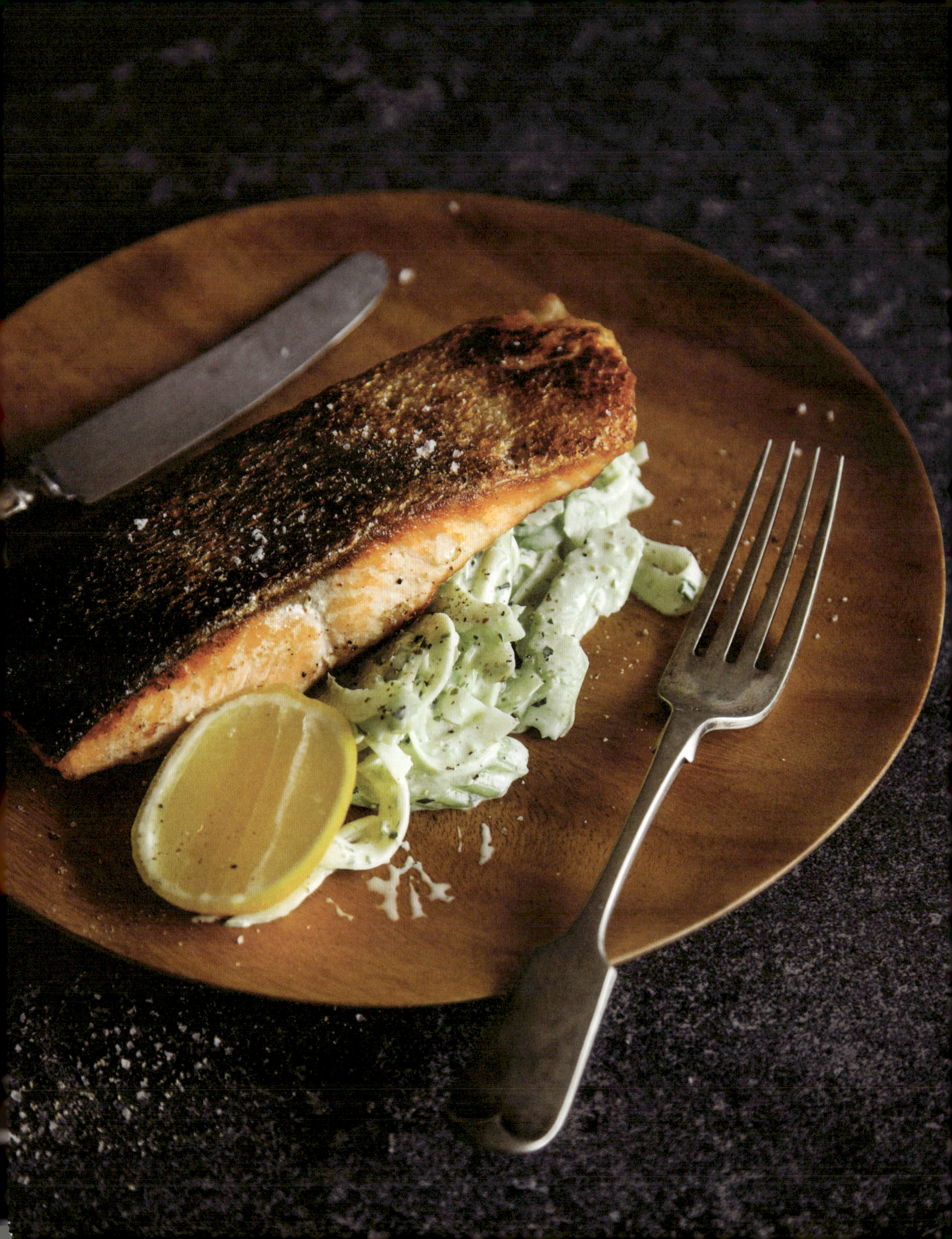

Crispy Skin Salmon with Fennel & Celery Remoulade

SERVES 4

4 x 200 g skin-on salmon fillets
lemon cheeks, to serve

FENNEL & CELERY REMOULADE

3 tablespoons whole egg mayonnaise
60 g (¼ cup) Greek-style yoghurt
1 teaspoon dijon mustard
1 tablespoon finely chopped flat-leaf parsley
1 tablespoon finely chopped chives
2 teaspoons finely chopped tarragon
1 tablespoon roughly chopped capers
2 cornichons, finely chopped
2 fennel bulbs, halved lengthways, cored and shaved
2 celery stalks, thinly sliced on the diagonal

To make the remoulade, combine the mayonnaise, yoghurt and mustard in a large mixing bowl. Add the parsley, chives, tarragon, capers and cornichons and stir thoroughly. Mix in the fennel and celery and season with pepper to taste. Cover with plastic wrap and refrigerate until required.

Preheat a barbecue hotplate to high and lightly grease with oil.

Pat the salmon skin dry with paper towel and sprinkle generously with salt. Cover and allow to rest for 20 minutes to bring to room temperature. The salt will cause the salmon skin to release moisture so pat dry again and sprinkle with a little more salt before cooking.

Cook the salmon skin-side down for 4 minutes until crisp and golden. Turn the fillets and cook for another 1–2 minutes, depending on the thickness of the fillets, until medium rare.

Serve the salmon with the remoulade and lemon cheeks.

LAMB

MOROCCAN LAMB MEATBALLS WITH MINTED YOGHURT
page 82

**GRILLED LAMB LOIN WITH ANCHOVY
& GARLIC BUTTER**
page 85

SPICY KASHMIRI ROAST LAMB
page 86

RACK OF LAMB WITH ROSEMARY CRUST
page 87

GREEK-STYLE SLOW-COOKED LAMB ROAST
page 88

MINT & GARLIC LAMB KEBABS WITH QUINOA TABOULI
page 91

TANDOORI-STYLE LAMB CUTLETS
page 92

LAMB CHOPS WITH PRESERVED LEMON GREMOLATA
page 93

**CHERMOULA LAMB SHOULDER WITH
GARLIC & TAHINI YOGHURT**
page 94

Moroccan Lamb Meatballs with Minted Yoghurt

SERVES 4–6

Unleavened grilled flatbread (page 137), to serve
½ red onion, finely sliced
chopped mint, to serve
chopped flat-leaf parsley, to serve
halved cherry tomatoes, to serve

MOROCCAN MEATBALLS

1 tablespoon ground cumin
1 tablespoon sweet paprika
4 garlic cloves, finely chopped
1 teaspoon sea salt flakes
½ cup coriander leaves, chopped
juice of ½ lemon
1 egg
2 tablespoons olive oil
2 tablespoons pine nuts, lightly toasted and roughly chopped
1 kg minced lamb

MINTED YOGHURT

250 g (1 cup) natural yoghurt
pinch of sugar
1 tablespoon finely chopped mint

To prepare the meatballs, combine the cumin, paprika, garlic, salt, coriander, lemon juice, egg, olive oil and pine nuts in a large mixing bowl. Add the lamb and mix well using your hands. Using wet hands, roll the mixture into golf ball-sized balls and flatten slightly into thick patties. Place on a tray, cover with plastic wrap and refrigerate for 1 hour.

Preheat a barbecue hotplate to medium and lightly grease with oil.

To make the minted yoghurt, combine the ingredients in a bowl.

Cook the meatballs, turning occasionally, for about 7–8 minutes until cooked through.

Toast the flatbreads on one side only for 20 seconds until warmed through and a little charred in places.

Serve by loading each uncharred side of the flatbread with onion, mint, parsley, tomato, a few meatballs and then drizzling with minted yoghurt.

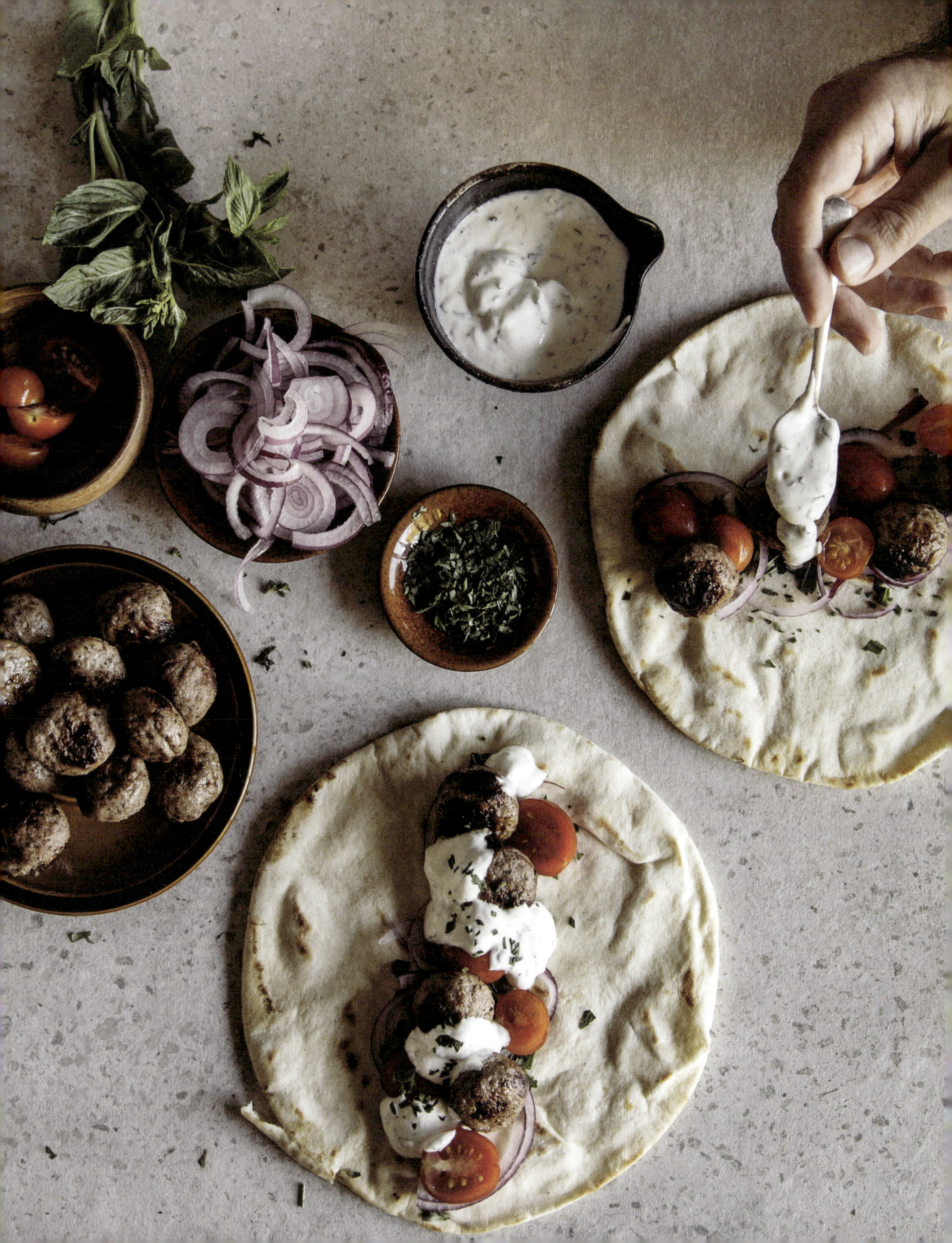

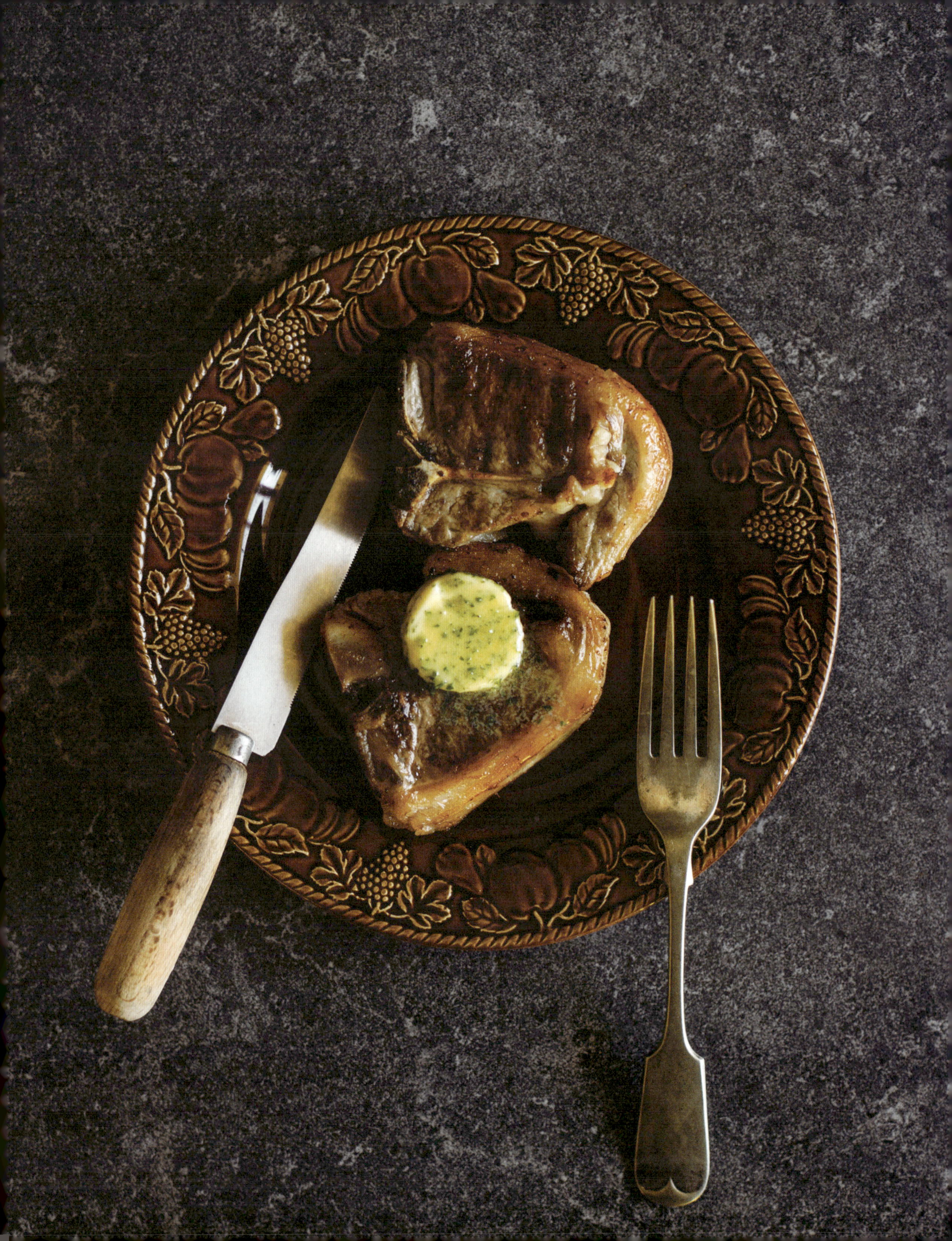

Grilled Lamb Loin with Anchovy & Garlic Butter

SERVES 4

2 tablespoons olive oil
½ teaspoon sea salt flakes
2 rosemary sprigs, roughly chopped
8 thick lamb loin chops

ANCHOVY & GARLIC BUTTER
6 anchovies, finely chopped
2 garlic cloves, crushed
2 tablespoons finely chopped flat-leaf parsley
zest of ½ lemon
125 g butter, softened

To make the butter, pound the anchovies, garlic, parsley and lemon zest to a paste using a mortar and pestle. Combine with the butter and mix well. Lay a sheet of baking paper on a work surface and spoon the butter into a thick line in the centre. Roll into a log and chill until needed.

In a small bowl, combine the oil, salt and rosemary. Brush the lamb chops with the oil, cover with plastic wrap and set aside for 30 minutes to come to room temperature.

Preheat a barbecue grill to high and lightly grease with oil.

Cook the lamb chops for 3–4 minutes on each side for medium, or 4–5 minutes on each side for well done. Transfer to a plate, cover loosely with foil and rest for 5 minutes.

Slice the anchovy butter into discs and serve on the lamb chops.

SPICY KASHMIRI ROAST LAMB

SERVES 6

1.5 kg butterflied boneless lamb leg
125 g (½ cup) natural yoghurt
150 g (½ cup) almonds
1 tablespoon honey

KASHMIRI SPICE MIX
2 cm piece of ginger, grated
4 garlic cloves, crushed
1 small red chilli, finely chopped
1½ teaspoons sea salt flakes
1 teaspoon ground cumin
1 teaspoon ground turmeric
½ teaspoon ground cardamom
½ teaspoon freshly ground black pepper
juice of ½ lemon
2 tablespoons olive oil

Preheat a hooded barbecue grill to medium and lightly grease with oil.

To make the spice mix, combine the ingredients in a small bowl. Rub all over the lamb to coat well.

Blend the yoghurt, almonds and honey in a food processor until smooth. Coat the spiced lamb with the yoghurt mixture.

Place the lamb on the grill and cook, covered, for about 40 minutes, turning once halfway through. Cooking times will vary; if lamb is still rare, turn again and cook for a further 10–15 minutes or until cooked through. Remove from the heat, cover and rest for 15 minutes before slicing.

RACK OF LAMB WITH ROSEMARY CRUST

SERVES 4–6

- 2 racks of lamb, with 6–8 points on each rack
- 1 tablespoon olive oil, plus extra for brushing
- 2 garlic cloves, crushed
- 1 tablespoon wholegrain mustard
- zest of 1 lemon
- 2 sprigs fresh rosemary, finely chopped
- 2 tablespoons finely chopped flat-leaf parsley
- 1 tablespoon dry breadcrumbs

Cut the lamb racks in half, to make 4 racks of 3–4 cutlets each. Brush the racks with olive oil and season on both sides with salt and pepper.

In a small bowl, combine 1 tablespoon of olive oil with the garlic, mustard and lemon zest. Place lamb racks bone-side down on a tray and spread the mustard mixture evenly onto the fat side.

Combine the rosemary, parsley and breadcrumbs in a small bowl. Press the mixture firmly into the mustard to help it adhere. Set aside to rest for 30 minutes.

Preheat a hooded barbecue grill to medium high heat and lightly grease with oil.

Cook the lamb racks, crust-side down, for 3 minutes, then turn and cook for another 6 minutes. Lower the heat to medium. Stand the racks upright, leaning against each other to balance, then cover the barbecue and cook for 15–20 minutes or until done to your liking.

Remove the lamb from the heat, cover loosely with foil and rest for 10 minutes before slicing into cutlets to serve.

GREEK-STYLE SLOW-COOKED LAMB ROAST SERVES 6

4 rosemary sprigs
4 mint sprigs
8 oregano sprigs
1 small bunch thyme
4 lemon balm sprigs
1 lemon, sliced
6 garlic cloves, unpeeled
2.5 kg lamb leg
2 tablespoons olive oil
1 teaspoon sea salt flakes
½ teaspoon freshly ground black pepper
green salad and Summer veg ratatouille parcels (page 134), to serve (optional)

Preheat a hooded barbecue grill to low and lightly grease with oil.

Line a baking tin with baking paper and spread half the herbs, lemon slices and garlic over the bottom.

Rub the lamb leg with olive oil, salt and pepper, and place it on top of the herbs. Put the remaining herbs, lemon and garlic on and around the lamb.

Place the baking tin on the grill, cover and cook for up to 5 hours, until the lamb is caramelised and tender (cooking time will depend on the barbecue heat and the size of the roast). After cooking for 3 hours, check for doneness every 30 minutes, replacing the cover and continuing to cook if required.

Remove from the heat, cover in foil and rest for 20 minutes before carving.

This roast is great served with a simple green salad and Summer veg ratatouille parcels.

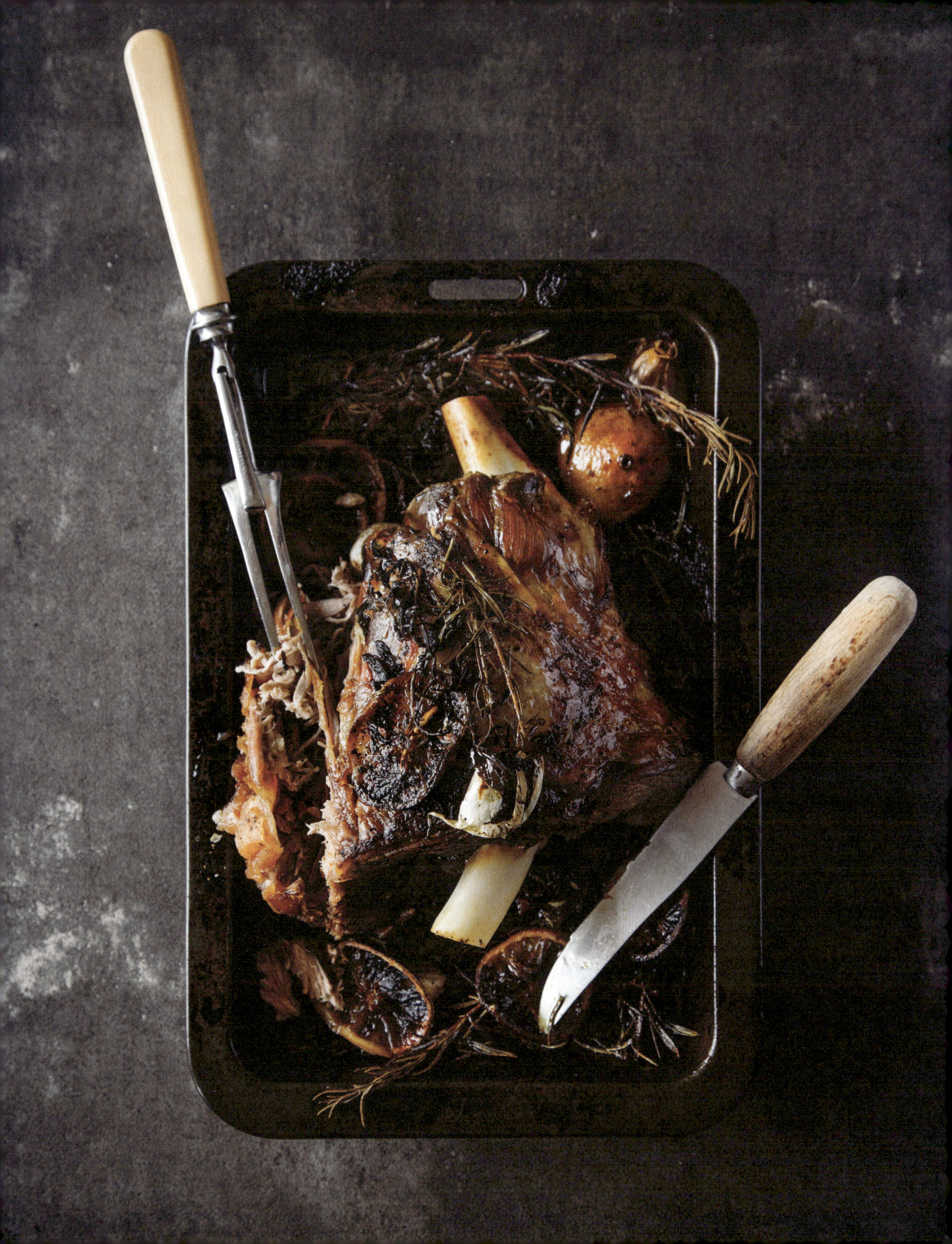

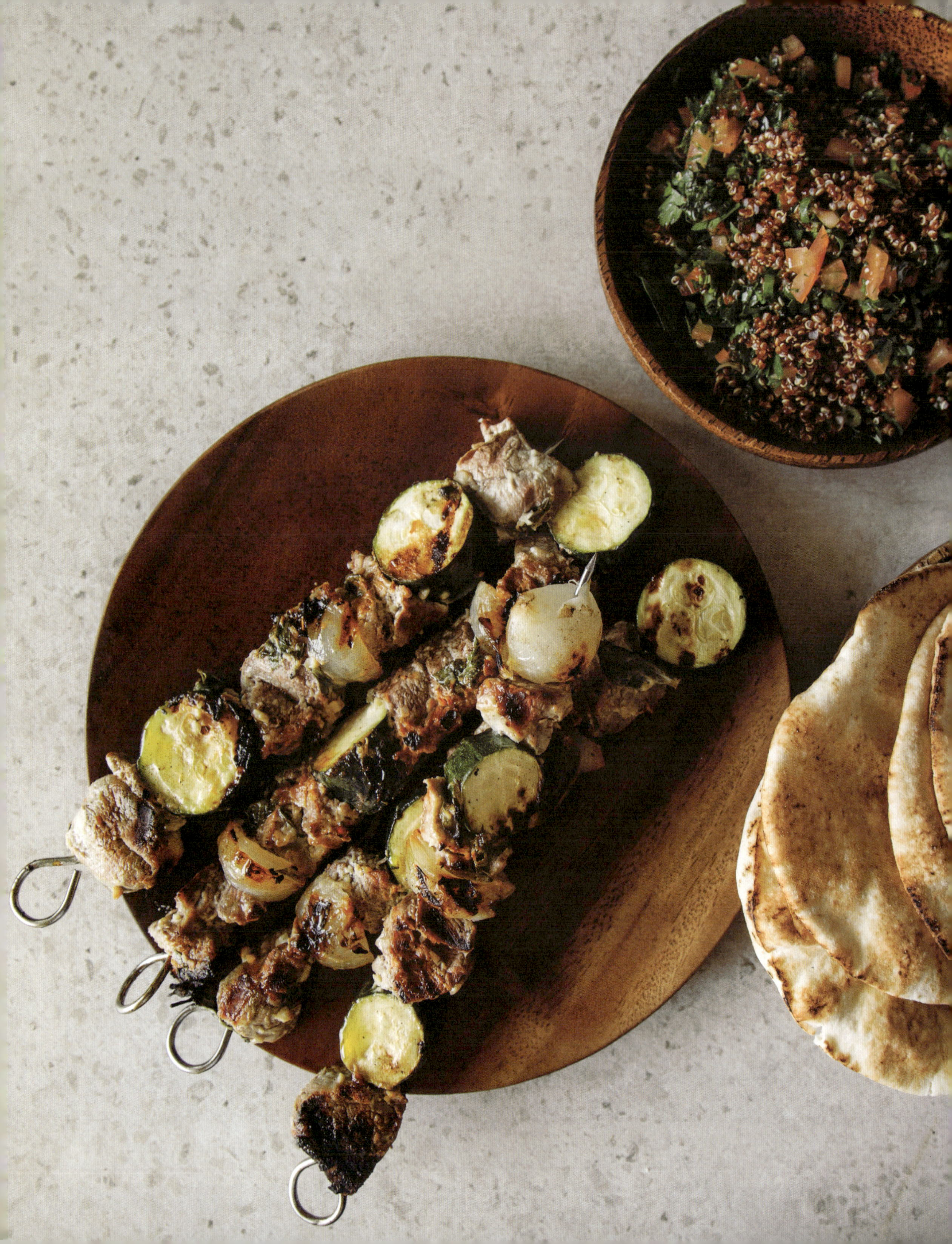

MINT & GARLIC LAMB KEBABS WITH QUINOA TABOULI

MAKES 10 SKEWERS

1 kg boneless lamb leg, cut into 5 cm cubes
10 tiny onions (pickling onions), peeled and halved
2 zucchini, cut into 2 cm rounds
Unleavened or Yeasted grilled flatbread (pages 136–137), to serve (optional)
Roasted chickpea & garlic hommus, (page 151), to serve (optional)

MARINADE

250 g (1 cup) natural yoghurt
2 tablespoons extra-virgin olive oil
2 garlic cloves, roughly chopped
zest and juice of 1 lemon
½ cup mint leaves
3 tablespoons flat-leaf parsley leaves
3 teaspoons sea salt flakes
1 teaspoon cracked black pepper

QUINOA TABOULI

100 g (½ cup) red quinoa, well rinsed
1½ cups flat-leaf parsley leaves, finely chopped
1 cup mint leaves, finely sliced
1 tablespoon chopped oregano
4 spring onions, very finely sliced
3 roma (plum) tomatoes, diced
80 ml (⅓ cup) lemon juice
80 ml (⅓ cup) extra-virgin olive oil

To make the marinade, blend the yoghurt, olive oil, garlic, lemon zest and juice, mint, parsley, salt and pepper until smooth using a blender or food processor.

Place the lamb in a large zip-lock bag and pour in the marinade. Seal the bag, pushing out as much air as possible. Massage the bag to ensure the lamb is well coated in the marinade. Refrigerate for 4–8 hours.

To make the tabouli, bring a small saucepan of water to boil and cook the quinoa over medium–low heat for 15 minutes or until tender. Drain and set aside to cool. Combine the quinoa, parsley, mint, oregano, spring onions and tomatoes in a large serving bowl. Whisk together the lemon juice and olive oil and season to taste. Pour over the quinoa mixture and toss well.

Preheat a barbecue grill to medium–high and lightly grease with oil.

Thread cubes of marinated lamb onto 10 flat metal skewers, alternating with pieces of onion and zucchini.

Cook the kebabs for about 8–12 minutes, turning, until browned all over and cooked through.

Transfer the kebabs to a platter and rest for 5 minutes. If desired, serve with Grilled flatbread and Roasted chickpea & garlic hommus.

TANDOORI-STYLE LAMB CUTLETS SERVES 6

12 lamb cutlets
lemon or lime wedges, to serve

TANDOORI MARINADE
2 teaspoons chilli powder
1 teaspoon ground cumin
1 teaspoon ground coriander
1 teaspoon turmeric
½–1 teaspoon salt
2 tablespoons vegetable or canola oil
2 tablespoons white vinegar
125 g (½ cup) Greek yoghurt

To make the marinade, combine the chilli powder, cumin, coriander, turmeric, salt, oil and vinegar in a dish that will comfortably fit the cutlets. Add the cutlets to the marinade and mix to coat well. Cover and refrigerate for at least 1 hour.

Preheat a barbecue grill to high and lightly grease with oil.

Cook the cutlets for 2–3 minutes on each side for medium, or 3–4 minutes on each side for well done. Transfer to a plate, cover loosely with foil and rest for 2 minutes.

Serve with the lemon or lime wedges for squeezing over.

LAMB CHOPS WITH PRESERVED LEMON GREMOLATA SERVES 6

60 ml (¼ cup) white vinegar
2 teaspoons salt
½ teaspoon freshly ground black pepper
1 teaspoon dried oregano
2 cloves garlic, crushed
2 tablespoons olive oil
6 lamb chump or shoulder chops

PRESERVED LEMON GREMOLATA
¼ preserved lemon, skin only, finely diced
1 small handful parsley, finely chopped
½ garlic clove, crushed

Combine the vinegar, salt, pepper, oregano, garlic and olive oil in a large dish that will comfortably fit the chops. Add the chops to the marinade and mix to coat well. Cover and refrigerate for at least 2 hours.

Preheat a barbecue grill to high and lightly grease with oil.

Cook the chops for 3 minutes on each side for medium, or 4 minutes on each side for well done. Transfer to a plate, cover loosely with foil and rest for 3 minutes.

Meanwhile, for the gremolata, combine the ingredients in a small bowl.

Serve the chops sprinkled with the gremolata.

CHERMOULA LAMB SHOULDER WITH GARLIC & TAHINI YOGHURT

SERVES 4–6

1 kg butterflied boneless lamb shoulder
chopped coriander leaves, to serve
chopped flat-leaf parsley, to serve

CHERMOULA

2 teaspoon cumin seeds
2 teaspoons coriander seeds
1 small onion, roughly chopped
3 garlic cloves, crushed
2 cm ginger, finely grated
zest and juice of 1 lemon
1 cup coriander leaves, roughly chopped
1 cup flat-leaf parsley leaves, roughly chopped
1 teaspoon smoked paprika
1 teaspoon salt
125 ml (½ cup) extra-virgin olive oil

GARLIC & TAHINI YOGHURT

125 g (½ cup) Greek-style yoghurt
juice of ½ lemon
1 tablespoon tahini
1 small garlic clove, crushed
¼ teaspoon ground cumin
sea salt flakes

To make the chermoula, toast the cumin and coriander in a small dry frying pan over medium heat for about 2 minutes until fragrant. Transfer to a food processor along with the remaining ingredients. Process until well combined.

Rub the chermoula all over the lamb shoulder, cover with plastic wrap and refrigerate for 2 hours or overnight.

Remove the lamb from the refrigerator 1 hour before cooking.

Preheat a hooded barbecue grill to medium–high and lightly grease with oil.

Cook the lamb skin-side down for 15 minutes. Turn and cook for a further 10 minutes. Reduce the heat to medium, cover and cook for a further 15 minutes. Remove from the heat, cover with foil and rest for 10 minutes.

To make yoghurt sauce, combine the ingredients in a small bowl.

Slice the lamb thinly, drizzle with the sauce and garnish with herbs to serve.

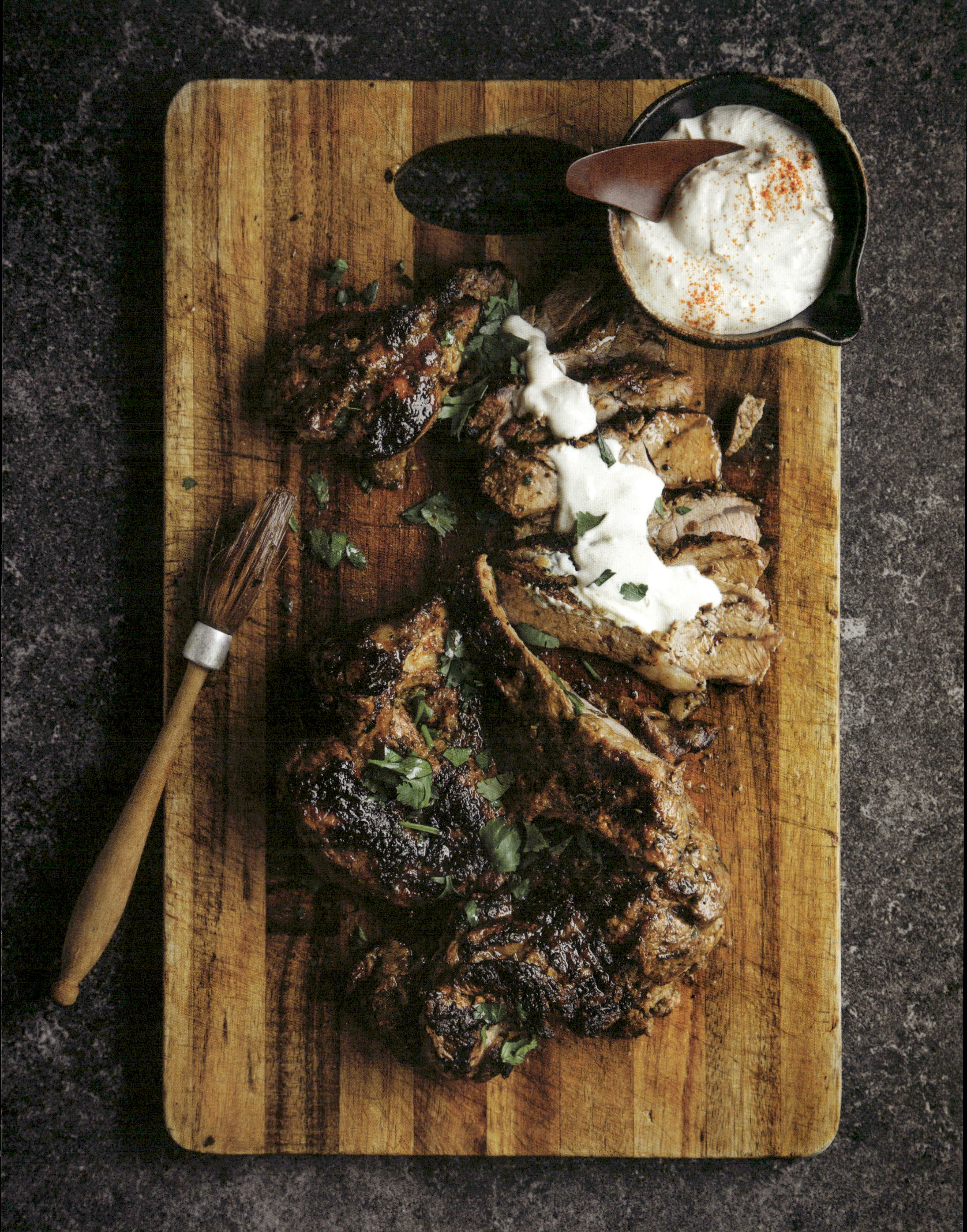

BEEF

BARBECUED STEAK WITH BÉARNAISE SAUCE
page 98

ARGENTINIAN BEEF WITH CHIMICHURRI
page 101

THE BOSS BEEF BURGERS
page 102

VEAL CUTLETS WITH SAGE, CAPERS & LEMON
page 104

RUMP STEAK WITH CORIANDER & JALAPEÑO BUTTER
page 105

STICKY BEEF SHORT RIBS WITH BOURBON-LACED BBQ SAUCE
page 107

THAI CHILLI–COCONUT SURF & TURF SKEWERS
page 108

GRILLED BEEF FAJITAS WITH SALSA & GUACAMOLE
page 111

Barbecued Steak with Béarnaise Sauce

SERVES 4

4 porterhouse steaks
Chargrilled witlof (page 145),
 to serve (optional)

BÉARNAISE SAUCE

250 g butter
2 French shallots, finely chopped
2 tablespoons white-wine vinegar
2 large egg yolks
1 tablespoon lemon juice, plus extra
 if required
1 tablespoon finely chopped tarragon
1 tablespoon olive oil

To make the béarnaise sauce, heat 1 tablespoon of the butter in a small saucepan over medium heat. Add the shallots and a grind of black pepper and cook for 30 seconds. Add the vinegar, reduce the heat to medium–low, and cook for about 2–3 minutes until the vinegar has evaporated. Reduce the heat to low and continue cooking for about 5 minutes until the shallots are tender and translucent. Transfer to a small bowl to cool.

Heat the remaining butter in a small saucepan over medium heat for about 2–3 minutes until it foams. Transfer to a small jug and keep hot.

Combine the vinegar reduction with the egg yolks, lemon juice, tarragon and 1 tablespoon of water in a small food processor and blend until smooth. With the motor running, add the hot butter in a thin, steady stream, discarding the milk solids in the bottom of the jug. Continue blending for 2–3 minutes until a smooth, creamy sauce forms. Pour the sauce into a medium-sized bowl and season to taste with salt, pepper, and more lemon juice, if desired. Cover and keep warm. Béarnaise sauce can be served at room temperature, but it is very tricky to reheat if you let it go cold.

Brush the steaks with oil and season both sides lightly with salt and pepper. Cover and set aside for 20 minutes to bring to room temperature.

Preheat a barbecue grill to high and lightly grease with oil.

When the grill is smoking hot, cook the steaks for 4 minutes on each side for medium rare (you can cook a little less or more according to your preference). Remove from the heat, cover and rest for 5 minutes.

Serve with the béarnaise sauce and, if desired, Chargrilled witlof.

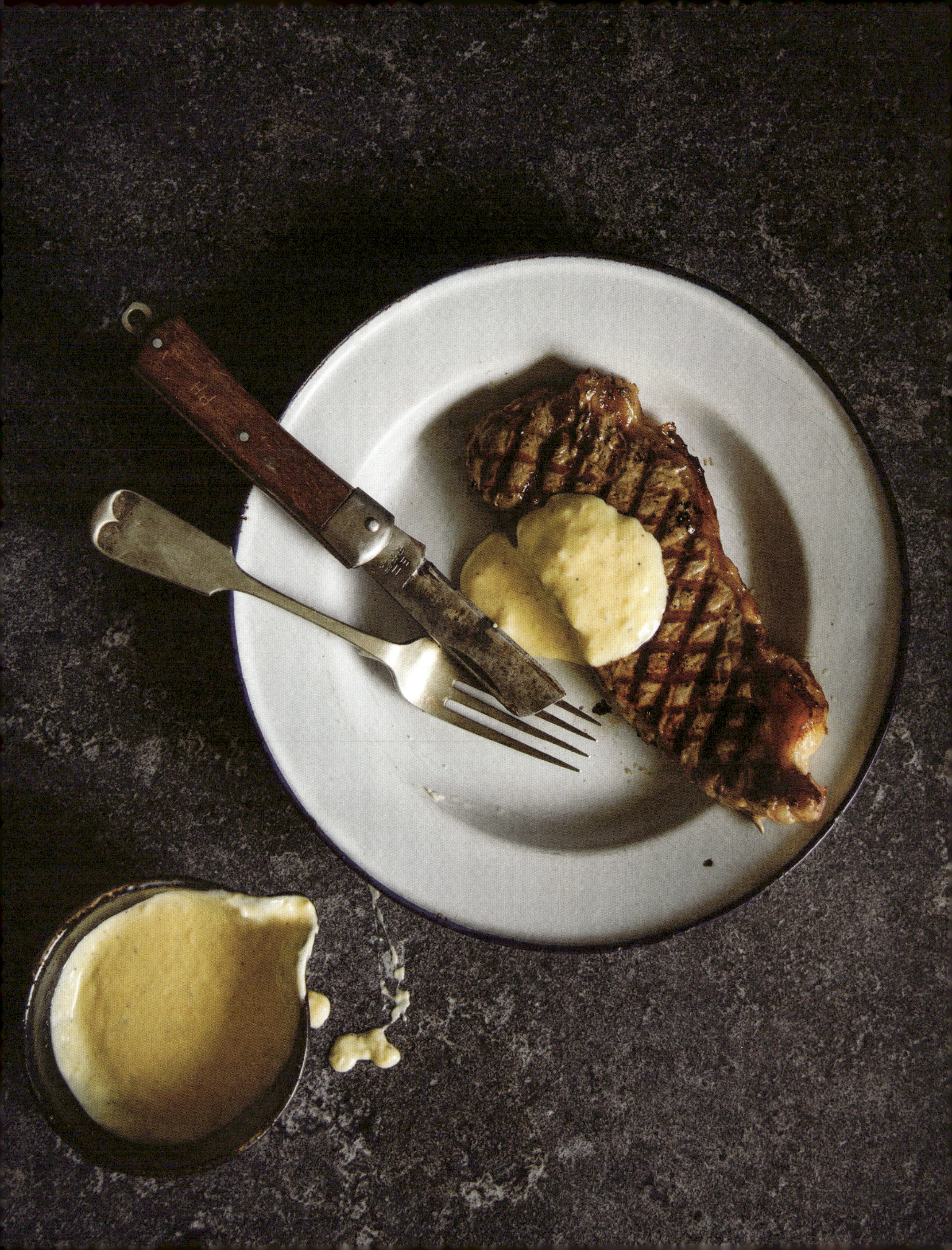

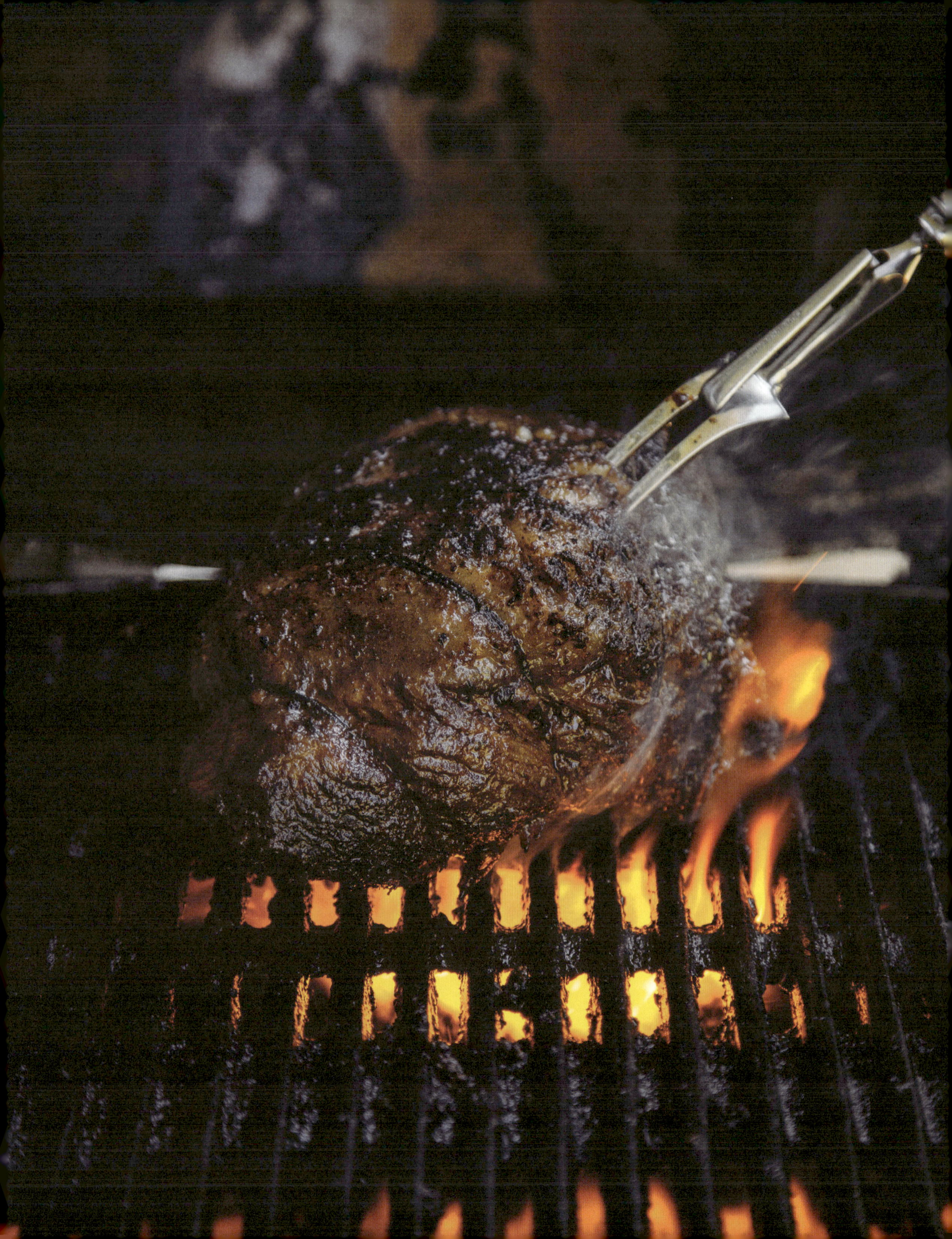

ARGENTINIAN BEEF WITH CHIMICHURRI

SERVES 6–8

2 kg beef rump, with fat cap intact

SPICE RUB

1 tablespoon smoked sweet paprika
1 tablespoon sea salt flakes
2 teaspoons ancho chilli powder
1 teaspoon soft brown sugar
1 teaspoon ground black pepper

CHIMICHURRI

2 cups flat-leaf parsley leaves, roughly chopped
1 cup coriander leaves, roughly chopped
½ cup mint leaves, roughly chopped
3 garlic cloves, roughly chopped
2 French shallots, roughly chopped
2 long red chillies, deseeded and roughly chopped
60 ml (¼ cup) lemon juice
2 tablespoons sherry vinegar or red-wine vinegar
1 teaspoon sea salt flakes
½ teaspoon freshly ground black pepper
185 ml (¾ cup) extra-virgin olive oil

To make the spice rub, combine the ingredients in a small bowl.

Place the beef on a clean work surface and, using a sharp knife, score the fat in a crosshatch pattern. Cut deeply, but don't cut into the meat. (This will help to baste the meat as it cooks by evenly releasing the flavoursome fat, and it will also stop the sides of the meat from curling.) Massage the spice rub deeply into the grooves and all over the meat. Cover with plastic wrap and refrigerate for 2 hours.

To make the chimichurri, blend the parsley, coriander, mint, garlic, shallots, chilli, lemon juice, vinegar, salt and pepper in a food processor until a coarse paste forms. With the motor running, add the oil in a thin, steady stream until incorporated. Taste and adjust the seasoning, then transfer to a small bowl, cover with plastic wrap and refrigerate until needed.

Preheat a hooded barbecue grill to high and lightly grease with oil.

Place the beef, fat-side up, onto the grill, cover and reduce the heat to medium–low. Cook for 45 minutes. Turn the beef and cook for a further 15 minutes. Turn again and for another 10 minutes for medium. (You can cook a little less or more according to your preference). Transfer to a plate, cover loosely with foil and rest for 20 minutes before slicing.

Slice the beef thickly and serve on a platter drizzled with half the chimichurri. Serve the remainder of the sauce in a small bowl for guests to help themselves.

THE BOSS BEEF BURGERS

SERVES 4

500 g minced lean beef
1 red onion, finely chopped
½ cup flat-leaf parsley leaves, finely chopped
¼ cup basil leaves, finely chopped
¼ cup semi-sundried tomatoes, finely chopped
1 egg
½ teaspoon sea salt flakes
¼ teaspoon ground black pepper
¼ teaspoon sweet paprika
4 round bread rolls, split
4 slices gruyère cheese
iceberg lettuce leaves, to serve
2 gherkins, sliced
1 large tomato, sliced
ketchup, mustard, mayonnaise, relish and/or chilli sauce, to serve

Combine the beef, onion, parsley, basil, sundried tomato, egg, salt, pepper and paprika in a large bowl. Mix well by hand. Divide in four even portions and, with wet hands, press into flat patties slightly wider than the bread rolls. Transfer to a plate, cover with plastic wrap and rest in the fridge for 30 minutes. (The patties will keep in the refrigerator for a few hours, so they can be prepared ahead of time.)

Heat a barbecue hotplate or grill to medium and lightly grease with oil.

Brush or spray the burgers lightly with olive oil. Cook, turning occasionally, for 10 minutes or until cooked through. When almost cooked, top each burger with a cheese slice to melt and then toast the buns lightly on both sides.

Spread the base of each bun with your sauce/s of choice then top with lettuce, gherkins, the burger and tomato slices. Spread the top with any other sauce, as desired, and dig in.

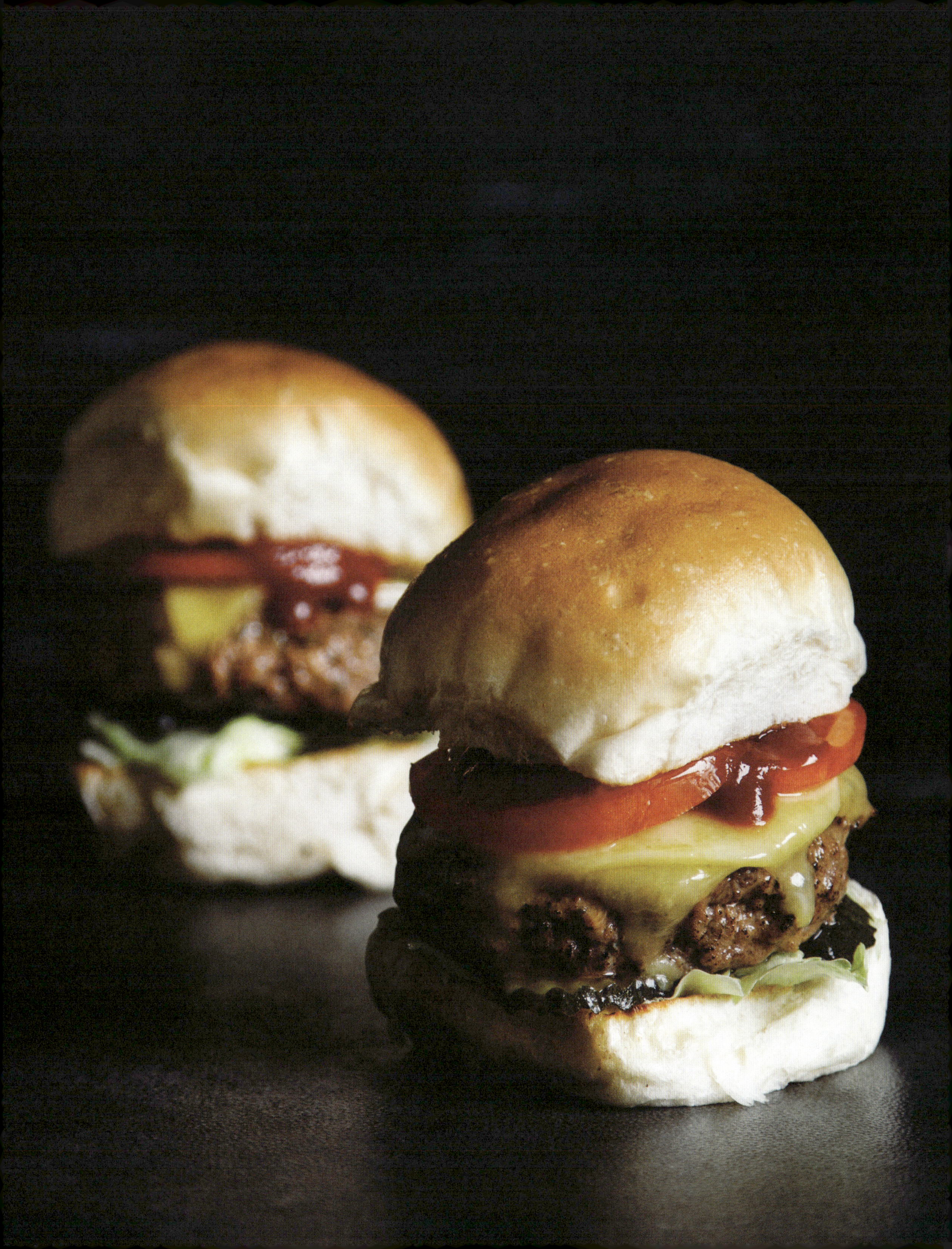

VEAL CUTLETS WITH SAGE, CAPERS & LEMON

SERVES 4

2 anchovies, roughly chopped
2 garlic cloves, finely chopped
1 tablespoon olive oil
4 x 250 g veal cutlets
2 lemons, halved
125 g butter, coarsely chopped
1 tablespoon capers, drained
20 sage leaves
2 tablespoons lemon juice

In a small bowl, mash the anchovies with a fork. Stir in the garlic and olive oil. Brush the cutlets on both sides with the anchovy mixture, cover and set aside for 30 minutes.

Preheat a barbecue grill to high and lightly grease with oil.

Cook the cutlets for 5 minutes each side or until caramelised on the outside. Cook the lemon halves, cut-side down, for 3–4 minutes until beginning to char. Remove the veal and lemons from the heat, cover and rest for 5 minutes.

Reduce the heat to medium and place a small frying pan on the grill. Add the butter, and cook, swirling the pan to melt evenly, until the butter begins to foam. Add the capers and sage and cook until crisp. Mix in the lemon juice and remove from the heat.

Serve the cutlets topped with the sage, caper and lemon butter and with the charred lemon halves for squeezing.

RUMP STEAK WITH CORIANDER & JALAPEÑO BUTTER

SERVES 4

4 rump steaks, about 200 g each
Mexican corn on the cob
  (page 143), to serve (optional)
lime wedges, to serve
coriander leaves, to serve

CORIANDER & JALAPEÑO BUTTER

80 g (⅓ cup) butter, softened
2 small jalapeño chillies, deseeded and finely chopped
¼ cup coriander leaves, finely chopped
zest of ½ lime
½ teaspoon sea salt

To make the butter, combine the ingredients in a small bowl, mixing well with a fork. Lay a sheet of baking paper on a work surface and spoon the butter into a thick line in the centre. Roll into a log and chill until needed.

Preheat a barbecue grill to high and lightly grease with oil.

Brush the steaks with olive oil and season lightly with salt on both sides.

When the grill is smoking hot, cook the steaks for 4 minutes on each side for medium rare (you can cook a little less or more according to your preference). Remove from the heat, cover and rest for 5 minutes.

Slice the butter into discs and serve on top of the steaks. Great accompanied by Mexican corn on the cob.

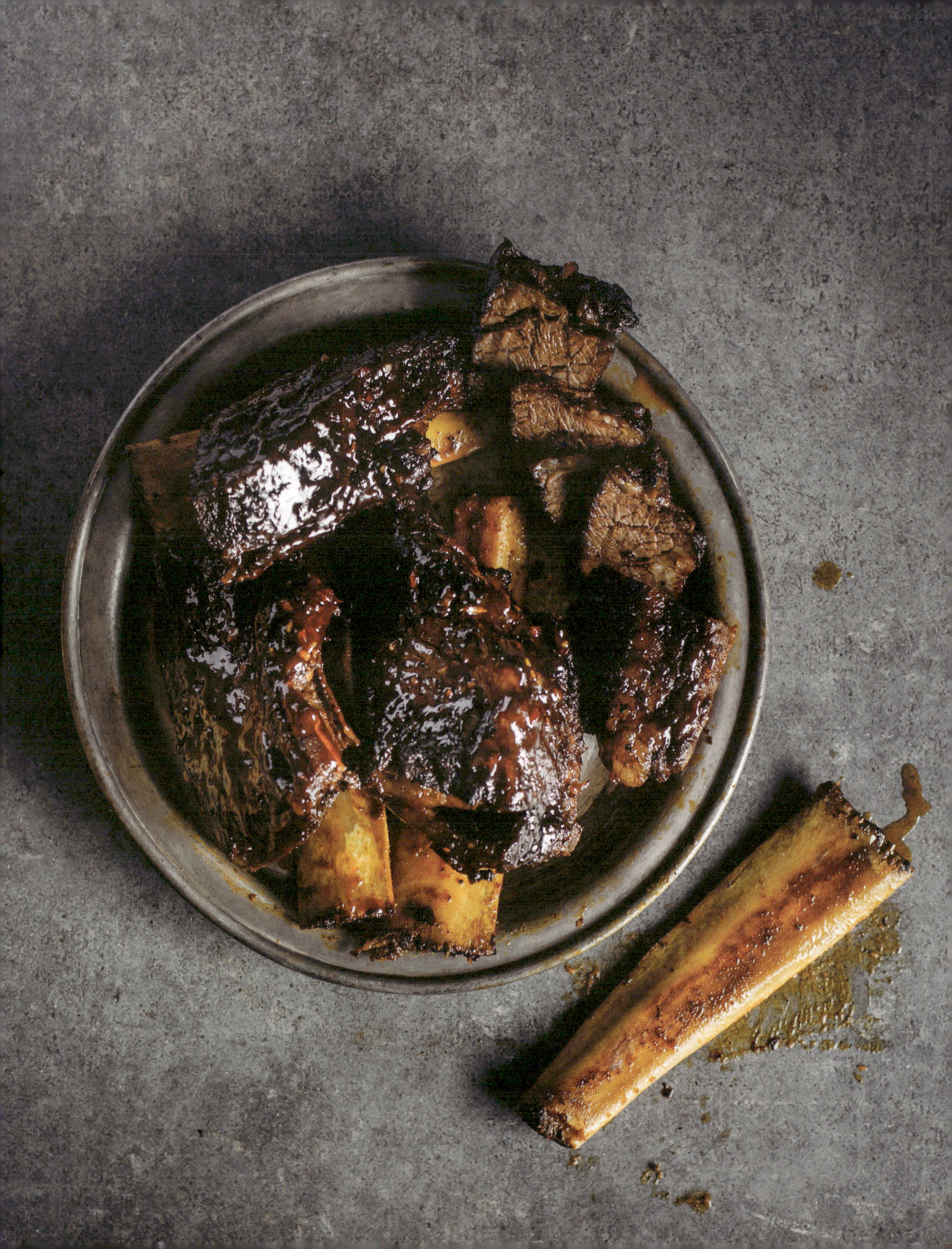

STICKY BEEF SHORT RIBS WITH BOURBON-LACED BBQ SAUCE

SERVES 4

2 kg beef short ribs, cut between bones into single ribs
Apple & cabbage slaw (page 144), to serve (optional)

SPICE RUB
1 tablespoon smoked paprika
2 teaspoons sea salt flakes
1 teaspoon freshly ground black pepper
3 garlic cloves, crushed
80 ml (⅓ cup) olive oil

BARBECUE SAUCE
2 tablespoons olive oil
1 onion, finely chopped
2 garlic cloves, crushed
1 long red chilli, deseeded and finely chopped
80 ml (⅓ cup) cider vinegar
45 g (¼ cup) soft brown sugar
170 ml (⅔ cup) tomato passata
2 tablespoons lemon juice
80 ml (⅓ cup) pure maple syrup
2 teaspoons dijon mustard
2 tablespoons worcestershire sauce
80 ml (⅓ cup) bourbon

To make the spice rub, combine the ingredients in a small bowl. Coat the ribs with the rub, massaging the seasoning in well. Cover with plastic wrap and refrigerate for 2 hours.

Preheat the oven to 150°C.

Place the ribs in a baking tin in a single layer. Cook for 2–2½ hours until tender.

Meanwhile, to make the barbecue sauce, heat the oil in a medium-sized saucepan over medium–low heat. Cook the onion, stirring occasionally for 8–10 minutes until softened. Add the garlic and chilli and cook for a further 4 minutes. Add the vinegar, sugar, passata, lemon juice, maple syrup, mustard, worcestershire sauce and bourbon. Stir to combine and bring to the boil. Reduce heat and simmer for about 15 minutes or until it develops a thick pouring consistency. Season to taste and set aside to cool.

Preheat a barbecue grill to medium high and lightly grease with oil.

Brush the ribs with barbecue sauce and cook, turning regularly and basting, for 20–30 minutes until a charred and sticky crust forms. Serve with remaining barbecue sauce and, if desired, Apple & cabbage slaw.

Thai Chilli-Coconut Surf & Turf Skewers

SERVES 4

24 large raw prawns, peeled, with tails left intact
300 g rump or sirloin steak, thinly sliced across the grain
bamboo skewers, soaked in cold water
cucumber slices, to serve
mint leaves, to serve
lime wedges, to serve

CHILLI-COCONUT MARINADE

300 ml coconut milk
2 lemongrass stalks, white part only, finely chopped
6 kaffir lime leaves, finely chopped
2 long red chillies, finely chopped
2 teaspoons grated palm sugar
zest and juice of 1 lime
2 tablespoons fish sauce
1 tablespoon kecap manis
2 tablespoons peanut oil

To make the marinade, combine the coconut milk, lemongrass, kaffir lime leaves and chilli in a small saucepan over low heat and simmer uncovered for 10 minutes. Set aside to cool to room temperature. Transfer to a food processor along with the palm sugar, lime zest and juice, fish sauce and kecap manis. Process until well blended. With the motor running, add the oil in a thin, steady stream until incorporated.

Divide the marinade between two large bowls, adding the beef and prawns to each separate bowl. Toss well to coat.

Thread the prawns and beef onto separate skewers, threading the prawns lengthways. Cover and refrigerate for 1 hour.

Preheat a barbecue grill to high and lightly grease with oil.

Cook skewers for 1–2 minutes each side or until just cooked through.

Serve with cucumber, mint leaves and lime wedges.

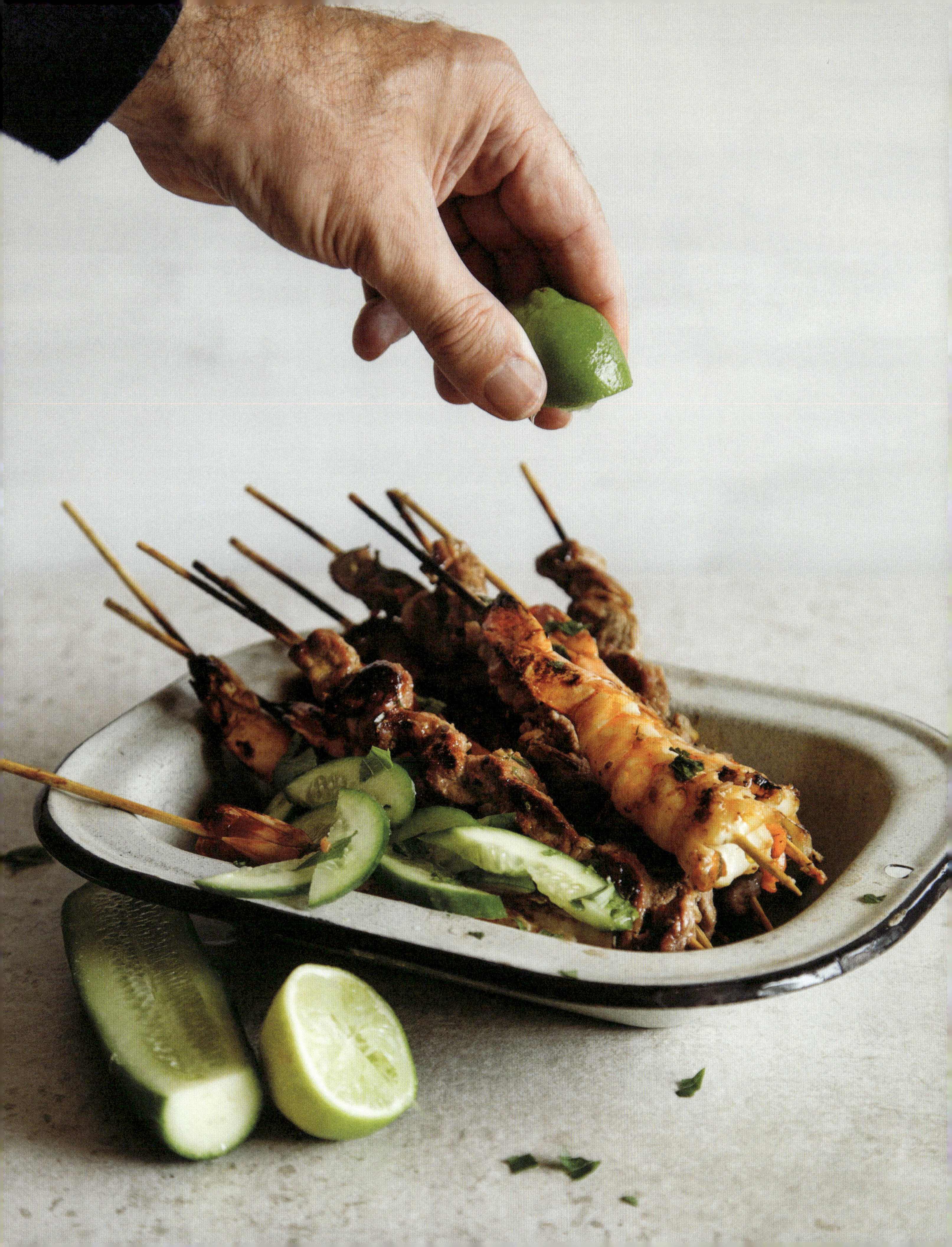

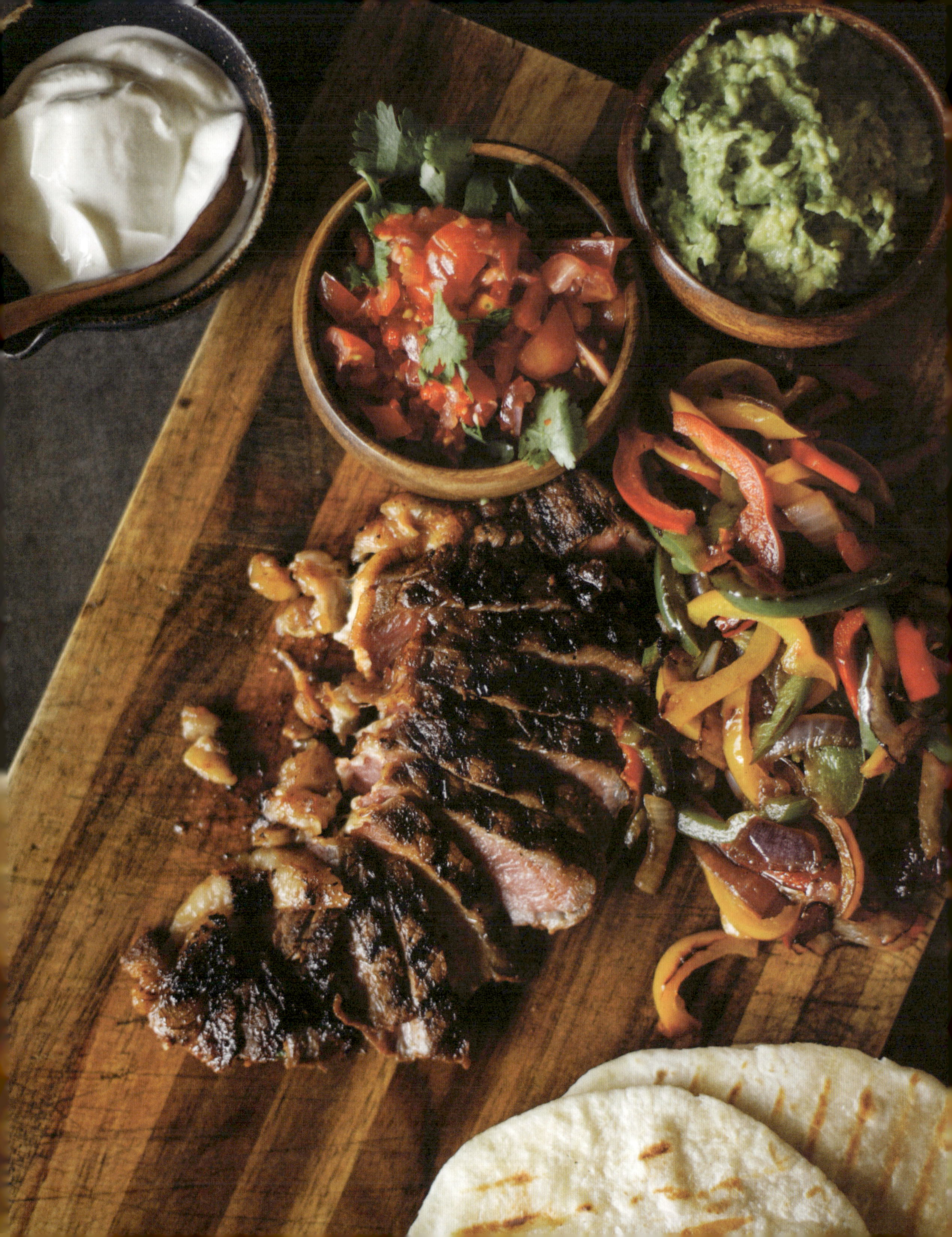

Grilled Beef Fajitas with Salsa & Guacamole

SERVES 4–6

1 kg beef skirt steak
2 red onions, halved and sliced
1 red capsicum, sliced
1 green capsicum, sliced
1 yellow capsicum, sliced
10 flour tortillas
150 g queso fresco or feta cheese, crumbled
125 g (½ cup) sour cream

MARINADE

125 ml (½ cup) olive oil
3 garlic cloves, crushed
3 tablespoons soy sauce
juice of 2 limes
1 tablespoon soft brown sugar
1 tablespoon ground cumin
2 teaspoons ancho chilli powder
2 teaspoons chilli flakes
1 teaspoon sea salt flakes
½ teaspoon freshly ground black pepper

FRESH TOMATO SALSA

1 long red chili, finely chopped
250 g cherry tomatoes, roughly chopped
1 cup coriander leaves and stalks, roughly chopped
juice of 1 lime

GUACAMOLE

1 avocado, peeled and diced
juice of ½ lime

To make the marinade, combine the ingredients in a small bowl and mix well.

Place the steaks in a dish and the onion and capsicum in a second dish. Divide the marinade between the dishes and mix to coat. Cover with plastic wrap and refrigerate for 2 hours.

To make the salsa, combine the ingredients in a small bowl. Season to taste. Cover and set aside until needed.

To make the guacamole, combine the ingredients in a bowl and mash roughly with a fork. Season to taste. Cover and set aside until needed.

Preheat a barbecue grill and hotplate to high and lightly grease with oil.

Cook the steaks on the grill for 1–2 minutes, then turn. Cook for another 1–2 minutes, and turn again. Continue cooking, turning every minute or so, for 8–10 minutes in total, or until done to your liking. Transfer to a plate, cover loosely with foil and rest for 10 minutes.

Cook the capsicum and onion mix on the hotplate, turning occasionally, for about 5–8 minutes or until just cooked and slightly charred. Transfer to a serving platter and keep warm.

Cut the steaks diagonally into thin slices and transfer to the serving platter.

Briefly toast the tortillas on one side over the hot grill and stack onto a board. Serve with the salsa, guacamole, cheese and sour cream alongside.

VEGGIE

HALOUMI BURGERS WITH PEPERONATA
page 114

GRILLED VEGETABLE & HALOUMI KEBABS
page 117

POTATO FRITTERS WITH APPLE SAUCE
page 118

GRILLED SPICED CAULIFLOWER STEAKS
page 119

MIXED MUSHROOM QUESADILLAS
page 120

JAPANESE OKONOMIYAKI
page 123

SOUTHERN-STYLE BARBECUED TOFU
page 124

HOMMUS & ZA'ATAR GRILLED VEGETABLE WRAPS
page 125

KOREAN BULGOGI TOFU
page 126

BARBECUED MEDITERRANEAN PIZZA WITH BASIL OIL & RICOTTA
page 129

EDAMAME BURGERS WITH RED ONION JAM
page 130

HALOUMI BURGERS WITH PEPERONATA

SERVES 4

1 tablespoon olive oil
250 g haloumi, coarsely grated
150 g sweet potato, coarsely grated
150 g zucchini, coarsely grated and squeezed to remove excess moisture
2 tablespoons finely chopped mint
2 tablespoons finely chopped flat-leaf parsley
finely grated zest of 1 lemon
1 large egg
4 wholegrain burger buns, split
1 large handful baby spinach or lettuce leaves
1 large tomato, sliced

PEPERONATA

2 tablespoons olive oil
2 garlic cloves, finely sliced
½ teaspoon dried chilli flakes
1 small red onion, finely sliced
2 red capsicums, sliced into 1 cm strips
¼ teaspoon sea salt flakes
½ teaspoon soft brown sugar

Heat the olive oil in a small frying pan over medium heat. Fry the sweet potato for 4–5 minutes until cooked and just beginning to caramelise. Set aside to cool.

In a large mixing bowl, combine the haloumi, sweet potato, zucchini, mint, parsley, lemon zest and egg.

Divide the mixture into four equal portions and, using wet hands, shape into patties. Cover with plastic wrap and refrigerate for at least 30 minutes to firm.

To make the peperonata, heat the olive oil in a medium-sized frying pan over medium heat. Add the garlic and chilli flakes, and cook gently for 1 minute. Add the onion and capsicum and cook, stirring frequently, for 15 minutes or until softened and beginning to caramelise. Add the salt and sugar and cook for a further 2 minutes.

Heat a barbecue hotplate to medium and lightly grease with oil.

Brush or spray the burgers lightly with olive oil. Cook on the hotplate for 3–4 minutes on each side until golden brown, using a barbeque spatula to gently turn the burgers.

Toast the burger buns lightly on each side, then assemble each with baby spinach or lettuce, tomato, a burger patty and the peperonata.

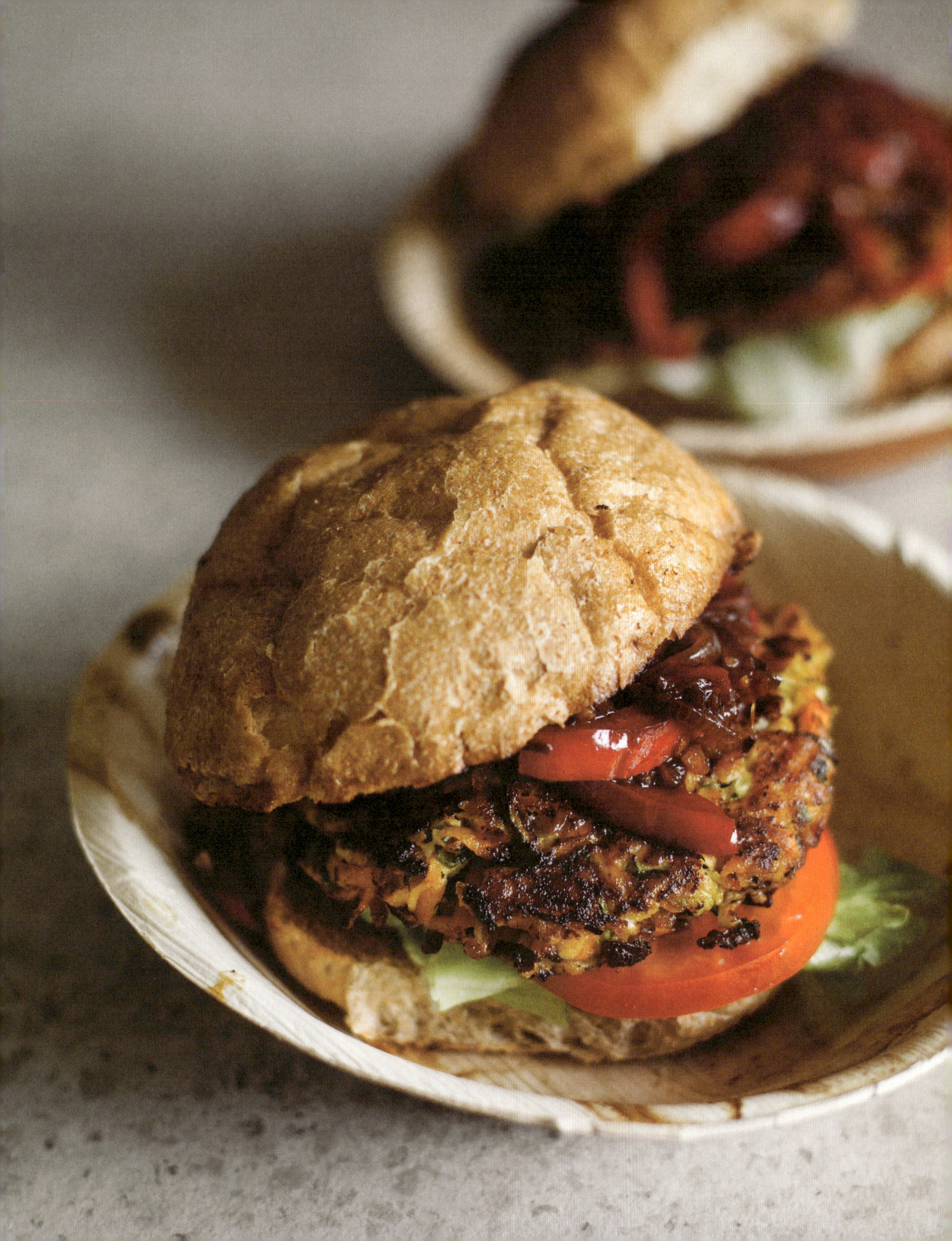

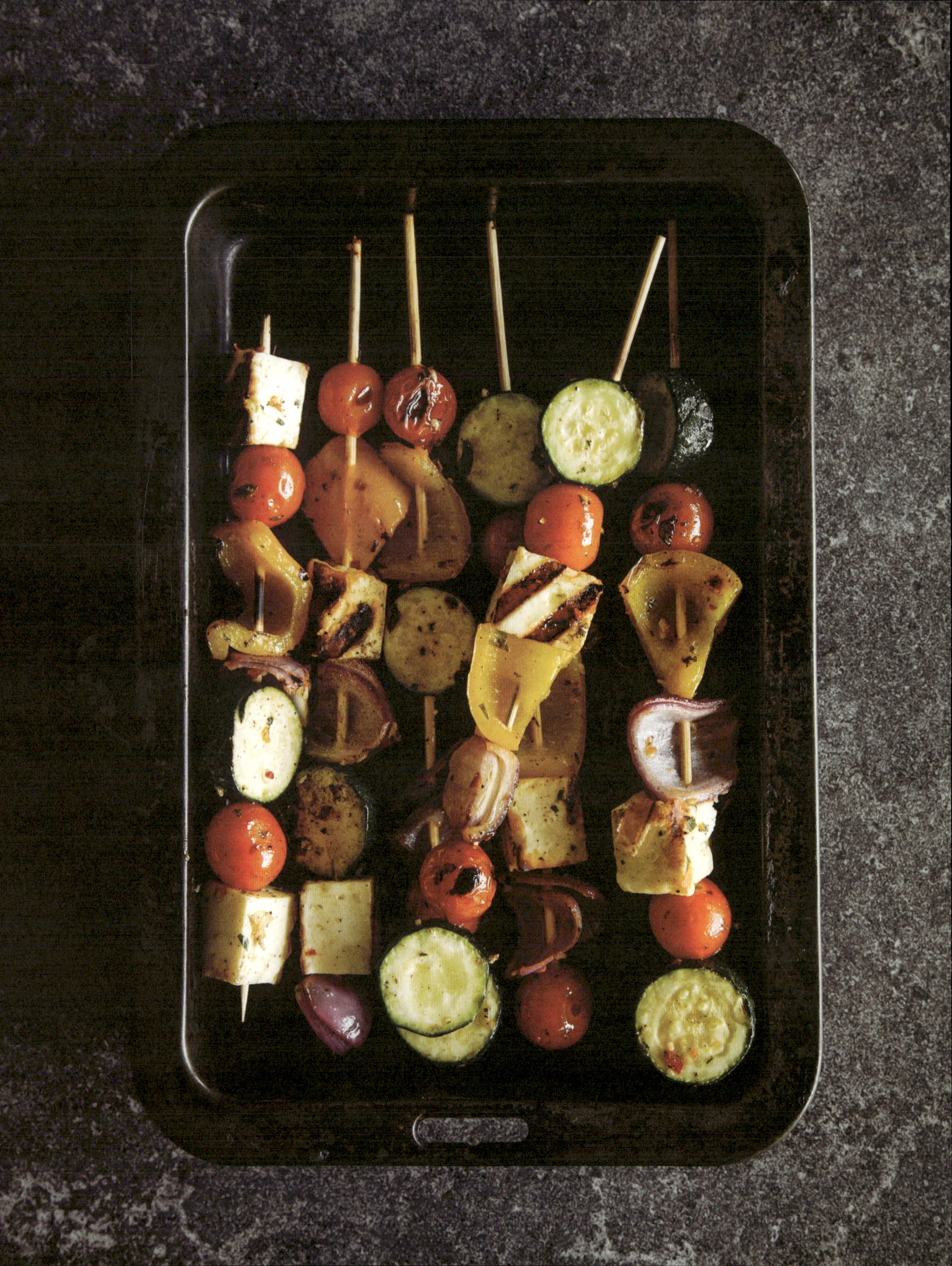

Grilled Vegetable & Haloumi Kebabs

SERVES 4

200 g haloumi, cut into 2 cm cubes
2 yellow capsicums, cut into 2 cm chunks
2 medium zucchini, sliced into 1 cm rounds
200 g cherry tomatoes
2 red onions, cut into 2 cm chunks
bamboo skewers, soaked in cold water
salad leaves, to serve
lemon wedges, to serve
Yeasted grilled flatbreads (page 136), to serve (optional)

MARINADE
60 ml (¼ cup) olive oil
juice of 1 lemon
2 garlic cloves, crushed
1 red chilli, finely chopped
8 mint leaves, finely chopped
1 tablespoon dried oregano

To make the marinade combine the ingredients in a large bowl and whisk well. Add the haloumi, capsicum, zucchini, tomatoes and onion, and toss to coat.

Preheat a barbecue hotplate to medium and lightly grease with oil.

Thread the haloumi and vegetables onto the skewers. Cook the kebabs for 3–5 minutes on each side until the haloumi browns and the vegetables have slightly softened and caramelised.

Serve with salad leaves, lemon wedges and flatbread (if desired).

POTATO FRITTERS WITH APPLE SAUCE

SERVES 4

450 g potatoes, peeled and grated
2 small onions, grated
¼ teaspoon salt
75 g (½ cup) plain flour
2 eggs, lightly beaten
1 tablespoon vegetable oil

APPLE SAUCE

550 g granny smith apples, peeled, cored and diced
¼ teaspoon ground cinnamon
pinch of salt
1 tablespoon sugar
squeeze of lemon juice

To make the apple sauce, place all of the ingredients and 80 ml (⅓ cup) water in a small saucepan over medium heat. Bring to the boil, then reduce the heat to low, cover and leave to cook for 15–20 minutes, until the apple has completely broken down. Remove from the heat and set aside to cool. If you would like a smooth sauce, place in a blender and blend until smooth. For a chunkier sauce, just mash with a fork until the larger chunks have broken down.

Preheat a barbecue hotplate to high and grease with oil.

Combine the potato, onion, salt and flour in a bowl. Add the egg and oil and mix well. Fill a ⅓ measuring cup with the potato mixture and place the mixture onto the hotplate. Flatten until the fritter is about 1 cm thick. Repeat this process, until you have 3–4 fritters on the hotplate. Fry for 4–5 minutes on each side, until golden brown and cooked through. Transfer to paper towel to drain, then repeat with the remaining mixture.

Serve the fritters with warm or cold apple sauce on the side. Any leftover apple sauce will keep in an airtight container in the fridge for up to 1 week.

Grilled Spiced Cauliflower Steaks

SERVES 4–6

2 large heads cauliflower, stalks trimmed
60 ml (¼ cup) olive oil
zest and juice of 2 limes
2 garlic cloves, crushed
2 tablespoons smoked paprika
1 teaspoon ground cumin
¼ teaspoon cayenne pepper
1 teaspoon salt
¼ cup finely chopped coriander leaves
lime wedges, to serve

Preheat a hooded barbecue grill to high and lightly grease with oil.

Cut the cauliflower into thick steaks (you should get 4–6 steaks – reserve the offcuts for another use).

Whisk the olive oil, lime juice and garlic together in a small bowl. In a separate bowl, combine the lime zest and the spices.

Brush one side of each cauliflower steak with the olive oil mixture and then sprinkle generously with the spice mixture. Place on the grill with the seasoned side down. Brush the tops with the olive oil mixture and season with the spice mix. Cover and cook for 5 to 6 minutes. Turn the cauliflower ande cook, covered, for another 5 minutes or until cooked through but still firm.

Serve sprinkled with chopped coriander and with lime wedges alongside.

MIXED MUSHROOM QUESADILLAS

SERVES 4

2 tablespoons olive oil
2 French shallots, finely chopped
3 garlic cloves, finely chopped
400 g mixed mushrooms (such as portobello, brown, king, porcini, oyster, button, shimeji), sliced
2 jalapeño chillies, finely chopped
½ teaspoon sea salt flakes
¼ teaspoon freshly ground pepper
8 soft corn tortillas, taco size
1 cup grated cheese such as queso fresco, mozzarella, fontina, cotija or parmesan
⅓ cup coriander leaves, finely chopped, plus extra to garnish

Preheat a barbecue hotplate to medium and lightly grease with oil.

In a large mixing bowl combine the olive oil, shallots, garlic, mushrooms, chillies, salt and pepper.

Cook on the hotplate, turning and stirring regularly, for 5–6 minutes, until the mushrooms and shallots become soft and begin to caramelise. Remove from the heat and set aside to cool slightly.

Top four tortillas with the mushroom mixture. Scatter the cheese and coriander over and top with a second tortilla. Place onto the hotplate and cook on both sides until golden brown and the cheese is melted.

Slice each quesadilla into quarters, garnish with coriander and serve.

Note: Quesadillas can be made from 1 tortilla folded in half to make a half moon, or 2 tortillas filled to make a circle as described above. The half moon shapes are great for kids as the fold reduces spillage.

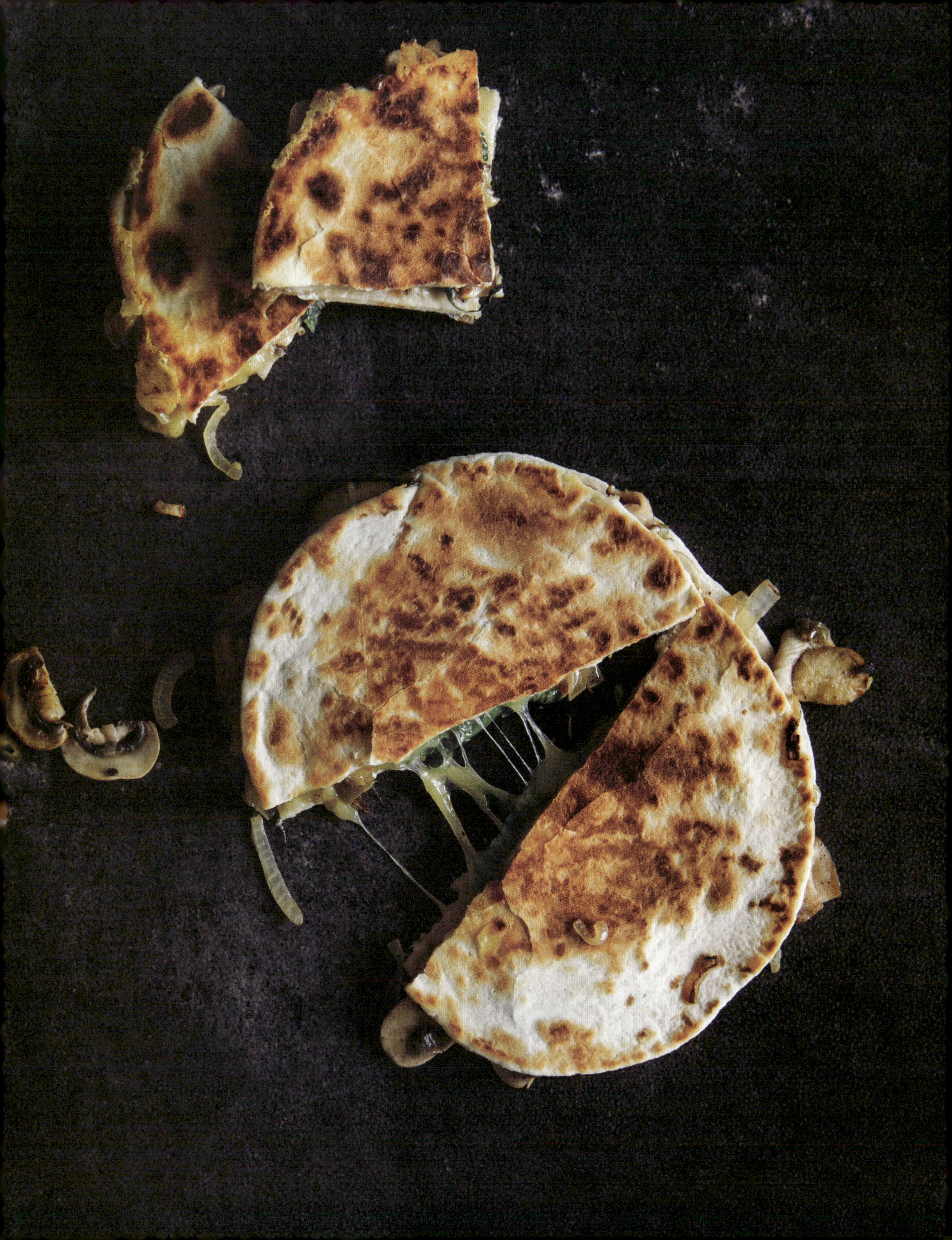

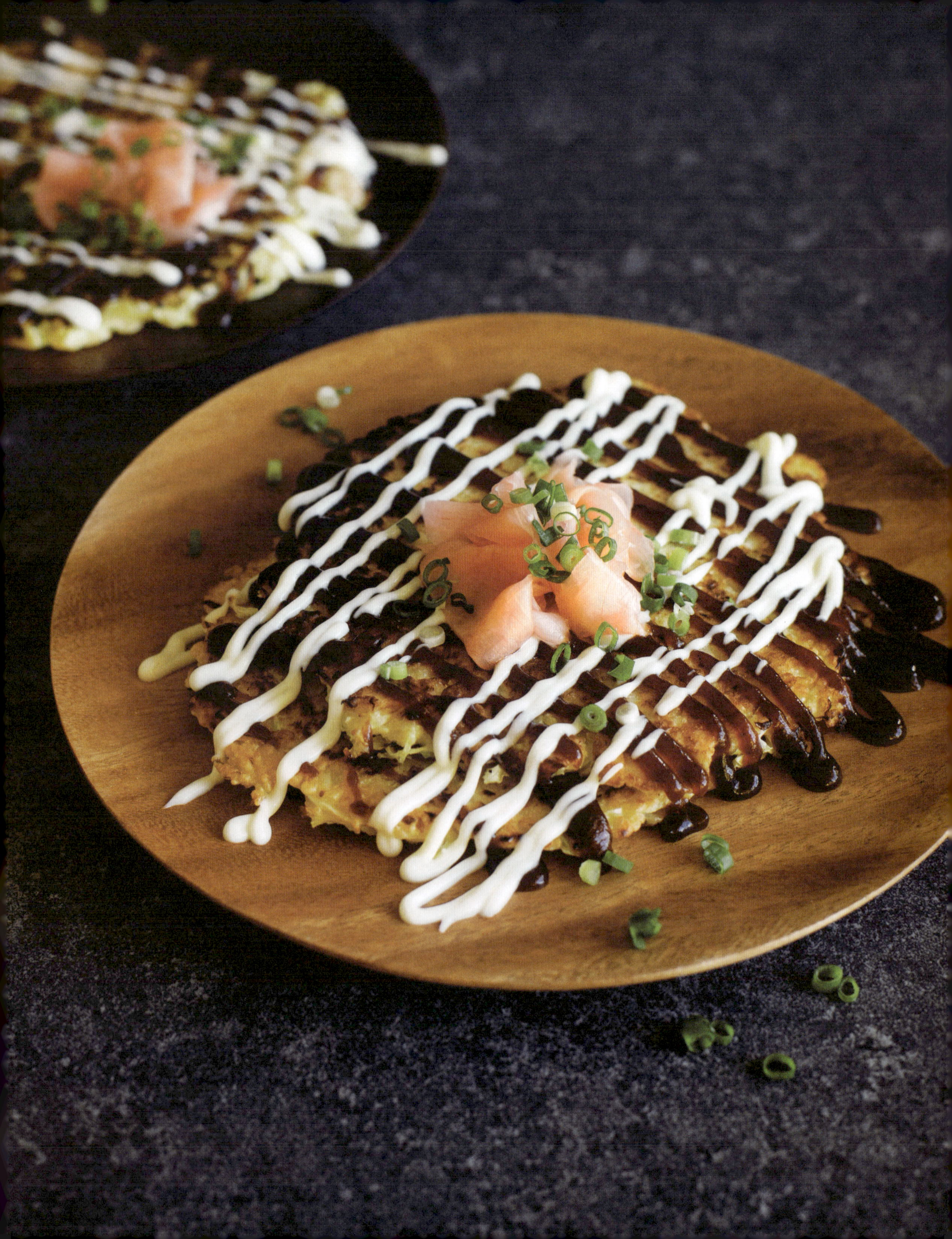

JAPANESE OKONOMIYAKI

MAKES 8

150 g (1 cup) plain flour
40 g (⅓ cup) cornflour
¼ teaspoon salt
¼ teaspoon sugar
¼ teaspoon baking powder
185 ml (¾ cup) vegetable stock
4 eggs
¼ cup pickled red ginger, plus extra to garnish
½ medium white or savoy cabbage, finely sliced
Okonomi sauce (see note), to serve
Japanese mayonnaise, to serve
8 spring onions, finely chopped

In a large bowl, combine the flour, cornflour, salt, sugar and baking powder. Add the stock, whisk well and refrigerate the batter for 1 hour.

Preheat a hooded barbecue hotplate to medium and lightly grease with oil.

Add the eggs and pickled ginger to the batter and mix well. Stir in the cabbage.

Pour ladles of batter onto the oiled hotplate to make eight pancakes. Cover and cook for 5 minutes until browned on the bottom. (The cover helps the thick pancake cook through to the centre.) Turn, cover and cook for 5 minutes until browned. Turn once more and cook, uncovered, for another 2 minutes.

To serve, drizzle with Okonomi sauce and Japanese mayo and garnish with spring onion and pickled ginger.

Note: Okonomi sauce is available from Asian grocery stores. A quick substitute sauce can be made by blending 3 tablespoons tomato ketchup, 1 tablespoon worcestershire sauce, 1 tablespoon soy sauce and 2 teaspoons of sugar.

SOUTHERN-STYLE BARBECUED TOFU

SERVES 4

2 blocks (600 g total) extra-firm tofu, cut into quarters then drained and dried
Apple & cabbage slaw (page 144), to serve (optional)

DRY RUB
1 teaspoon ground coriander
1 teaspoon ground cumin
2 teaspoons dried oregano
2 teaspoons sweet paprika
1 teaspoon smoked paprika
1 teaspoon garlic powder
1 teaspoon soft brown sugar
1 teaspoon ground cinnamon
2 teaspoons sea salt
1 teaspoon freshly ground black pepper

Preheat a barbecue grill to high heat and lightly grease with oil.

To make the rub, combine all of the ingredients in a small bowl.

Coat the tofu on all sides with the rub. Cook for about 4 minutes or until golden brown. Turn and cook for a further 4 minutes.

Remove from the heat and, if you like, serve with a side of Apple & cabbage slaw.

HOMMUS & ZA'ATAR GRILLED VEGETABLE WRAPS

SERVES 4

2 red capsicums, cut into 5 cm pieces
2 zucchini, sliced lengthways into 1 cm strips
2 eggplants, sliced into 1 cm rounds
1 red onion, sliced into rings
4 large flatbread wraps
Roast chickpea and garlic hommus (page 151), to serve
100 g baby spinach leaves
¼ cup mint leaves

ZA'ATAR MARINADE
1 tablespoon dried thyme
1 tablespoon sesame seeds
2 teaspoons sumac
½ teaspoon salt
60 ml (¼ cup) olive oil
juice of ½ lemon

Preheat a barbecue hotplate and grill to medium and lightly grease with oil.

To make the za'atar marinade, combine the ingredients in a large bowl and whisk well.

Brush the capsicum, zucchini and eggplant with the marinade then place on the grill. Cook, turning once, for 4–6 minutes. Toss the onion in the remaining marinade and cook on the hotplate for 8–10 minutes until tender and beginning to caramelise.

Toast the wraps on the grill briefly to soften.

Assemble the wraps by spreading each with a heaped tablespoon of hommus, and topping with a handful of spinach leaves, and the capsicum, zucchini, eggplant, onion and mint leaves before rolling up to serve.

KOREAN BULGOGI TOFU

SERVES 4

600 g firm tofu, drained and cut into cubes
½ onion, finely sliced
4 spring onions, finely sliced
12 iceberg lettuce leaves
2 cucumbers, cut into short spears
2 tablespoons sesame seeds, toasted

MARINADE
185 ml (¾ cup) tamari
½ onion, finely chopped
½ nashi pear, cored and grated
2 garlic cloves, crushed
1 teaspoon grated ginger
2 tablespoons soft brown sugar
1 teaspoon chilli flakes
½ teaspoon freshly ground black pepper
1 tablespoon sesame oil

To make the marinade, combine the ingredients in a small bowl.

Pour a little bit of marinade into the base of a dish, add the tofu, and pour the remaining marinade over. Cover and refrigerate for 20 minutes.

Preheat a barbecue hotplate to medium and lightly grease with oil.

Cook the onion, spring onions and tofu, turning the tofu after 4–5 minutes and continue cooking until caramelised.

Serve the tofu cubes in lettuce leaves with cucumber spears and sprinkled with sesame seeds.

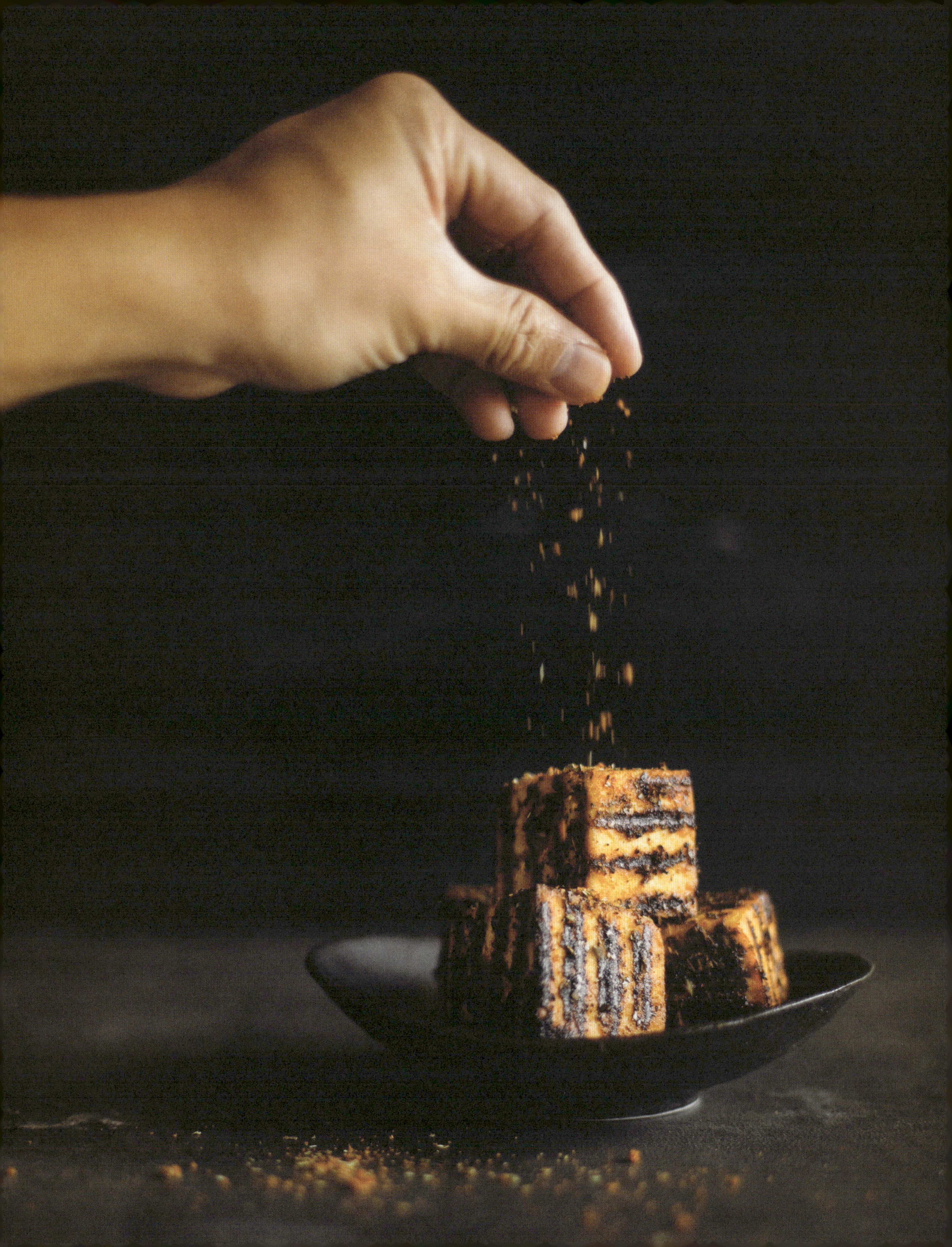

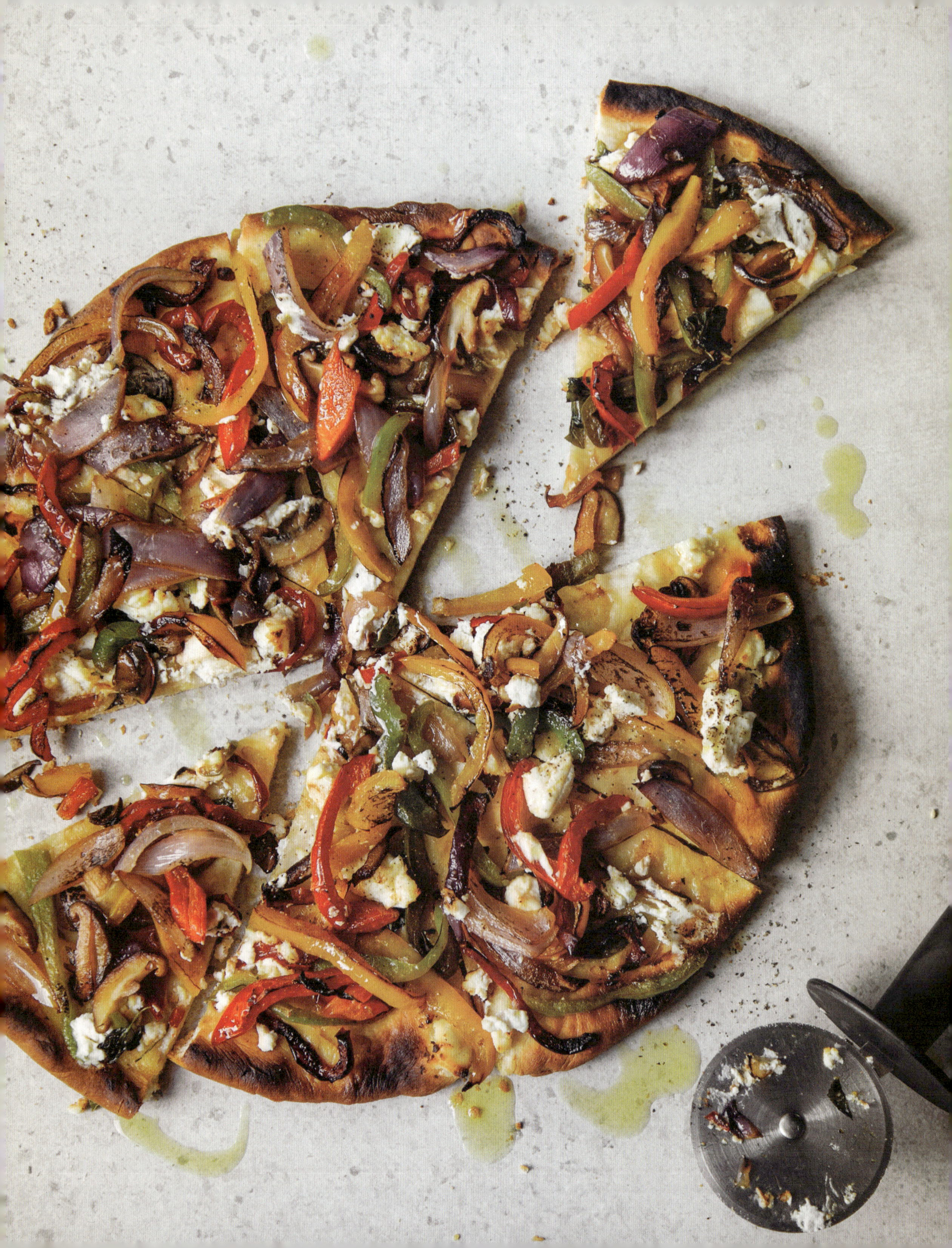

BARBECUED MEDITERRANEAN PIZZA WITH BASIL OIL & RICOTTA

SERVES 4

2 zucchini, cut diagonally into 1 cm slices
1 yellow capsicum, cut into strips
1 red capsicum, cut into strips
½ red onion, sliced into wedges
5 field mushrooms, sliced
200 g ricotta cheese
50 g (½ cup) grated parmesan cheese

PIZZA DOUGH

185 ml (¾ cup) warm water
½ teaspoon active dried yeast
350 g (2⅓ cups) strong flour
½ teaspoon sea salt flakes
3 tablespoons olive oil, plus extra for coating

BASIL OIL

60 ml (¼ cup) extra-virgin olive oil
½ cup basil leaves
2 garlic cloves, thinly sliced

To make the pizza dough, place the water in a small bowl and sprinkle the yeast over. Set aside for a few minutes until frothy. Combine the flour and salt in the bowl of an electric mixer fitted with a paddle attachment. Turn on to low speed and drizzle in the olive oil until combined. Slowly pour in the yeast mixture and mix until a sticky dough forms. Form the dough into a ball, cover with a little olive oil and place in a lightly oiled mixing bowl. Cover with plastic wrap and set aside in a warm place for 1–2 hours until the dough has doubled in size.

To make the basil oil, heat the oil in a small saucepan over medium-low heat. Add the basil leaves and garlic and swirl the pan until the leaves are wilted and the oil has become fragrant and turned a rich green colour.

Preheat a hooded barbecue grill to high and lightly grease with oil.

Brush the zucchini, capsicums, onion and mushrooms with half the basil oil. Grill, turning occasionally, until the vegetables are tender and have defined grill marks. Set aside.

In a small mixing bowl, mash the ricotta and parmesan together with a fork.

Lightly grease a 28 cm x 40 cm rectangular baking tray or two round pizza trays. On a floured surface, roll out the pizza dough to fit the tray or trays. Brush the remaining basil oil over the base, adding the basil leaves and garlic. Scatter spoonfuls of the cheese over the base, and arrange the zucchini, capsicums, onion and mushroom over the top.

Place the tray or trays over the barbecue grill and close the lid. Cook for about 10–15 minutes until the crust is golden brown.

EDAMAME BURGERS WITH RED ONION JAM

MAKES 6 REGULAR OR 10 MINI BURGERS

6 full-sized or 10 mini sourdough rolls
lettuce leaves, to serve
3 tomatoes, sliced
2 Lebanese cucumbers, sliced

RED ONION JAM

60 ml (¼ cup) olive oil
500 g red onions, thinly sliced
2 sprigs thyme
1 bay leaf
1 long red chilli, thinly sliced
2 tablespoons soft brown sugar
1 teaspoon sea salt flakes
¼ teaspoon freshly ground black pepper
2 tablespoons balsamic vinegar

EDAMAME PATTIES

80 g (½ cup) cashews
80 g (½ cup) grated carrot
1 small onion, diced
2 garlic cloves, roughly chopped
½ cup flat-leaf parsley leaves, chopped
1 tablespoon tamari
120 g (2 cups) podded edamame beans
110 g (1 cup) besan (chickpea flour)

To make the red onion jam, heat the oil in a medium-sized saucepan over medium heat. Add the onion, thyme, bay leaf and chilli. Cook, stirring regularly, for 25–30 minutes or until softened and golden. Add the sugar, salt, pepper, vinegar and 125 ml (½ cup) of water. Bring to the boil then reduce the heat to low. Simmer, uncovered, for 8–10 minutes or until thick and jammy.

To make the patties, blend the cashews, carrot, onion, garlic, parsley, tamari and half the edamame in a food processor until it forms a chunky paste. Transfer to a large bowl. Add remaining the beans and the besan, season to taste and mix well. Cover with plastic wrap and refrigerate for 30 minutes (this will make it easier to handle when forming the patties).

Preheat a barbecue hotplate to medium and lightly grease with oil.

Form the edamame mix into 6 or 10 patties and cook for 4–5 minutes each side or until golden.

Place the lettuce and patties on the rolls and top with tomato, cucumber and red onion jam.

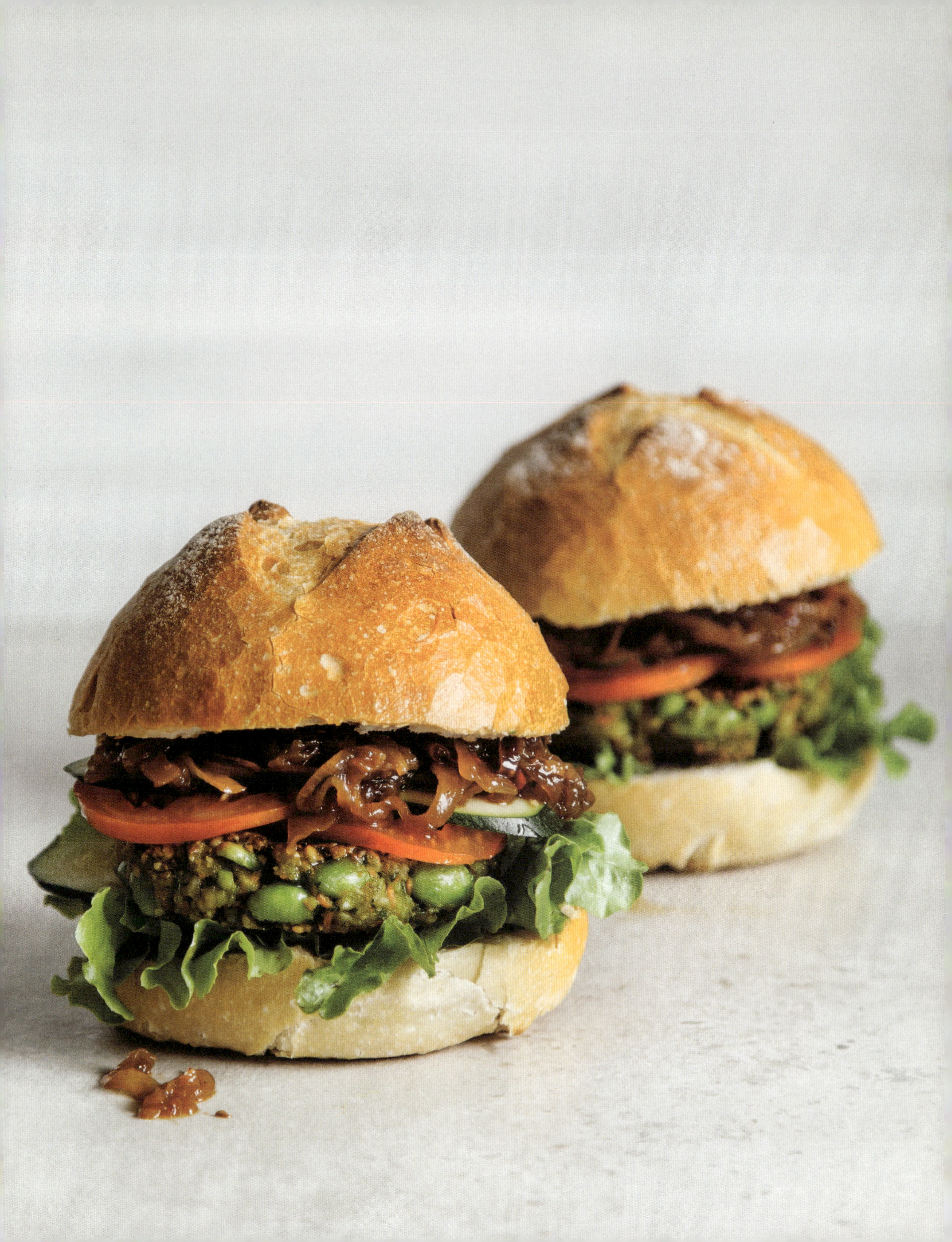

SIDES & SALADS

SUMMER VEG RATATOUILLE PARCELS
page 134

YEASTED GRILLED FLATBREAD
page 136

UNLEAVENED GRILLED FLATBREAD
page 137

BARBECUED POTATO WEDGES WITH LIME YOGHURT
page 140

HERBY NEW POTATO SALAD
page 141

MEXICAN CORN ON THE COB
page 143

APPLE & CABBAGE SLAW
page 144

CHARGRILLED WITLOF
page 145

FRESH CORN, BACON, KALE & JALAPEÑO SALAD
page 146

PORTUGUESE SALAD
page 149

GRILLED EGGPLANT WITH SAGE OIL
page 150

ROASTED CHICKPEA & GARLIC HOMMUS
page 151

GRILLED CAULIFLOWER & SWEET POTATO SALAD
page 152

BARBECUED BAKED POTATOES
pages 154–155

GERMAN POTATO SALAD
page 158

CUCUMBER SALAD
page 159

MEXICAN QUINOA SALAD
page 161

TURKISH ROASTED TOMATO SALAD
page 162

HOMEMADE TOMATO KETCHUP
page 163

GRILLED CABBAGE SALAD
page 164

WHITE BEAN SALAD WITH FRESH HERBS
page 166

CELERIAC REMOULADE
page 167

Summer Veg Ratatouille Parcels

SERVES 4–6 AS A SIDE

2 red onions, halved and thickly sliced
4 garlic cloves, unpeeled
1 eggplant, sliced into 1 cm rounds
2 zucchini, cut lengthways into 1 cm strips
2 red capsicums, halved and cut into strips
80 ml (⅓ cup) extra-virgin olive oil
½ teaspoon sea salt flakes
½ teaspoon freshly ground black pepper
4 thyme sprigs, leaves removed
500 g tomatoes, deseeded and diced
2 teaspoons balsamic vinegar
basil leaves, to garnish

Preheat a barbecue hotplate and grill to medium and lightly grease with oil.

In two separate bowls, toss the onion and garlic, and the eggplant, zucchini and capsicum in the olive oil.

Cook the onion and garlic on the hotplate, and the eggplant, zucchini and capsicum on the grill. Cook for 6–8 minutes, turning occasionally, until softened and caramelised.

Transfer to a mixing bowl along with the salt, pepper, thyme, tomatoes and balsamic vinegar. Toss to combine well.

Tear four 1 metre sheets of foil, and fold in half to make a double layer. Cut sheets of baking paper slightly smaller than the foil to place on top.

Use a slotted spoon to divide the vegetables evenly between the four sheets, placing the vegetables into the centre of each. Lift the sides up and seal along the side edges by folding over twice (about 2 cm for each fold), leaving the tops open.

Divide the remaining juices from the bowl between the parcels, then fold the tops to seal, folding twice as before, but ensuring you leave some room for steam.

Reduce the barbecue heat to low and cook the parcels on the grill for 20 minutes.

Vegetable parcels can be served hot or at room temperature, garnished with basil leaves. Be careful when opening the foil parcels as the steam inside will be very hot.

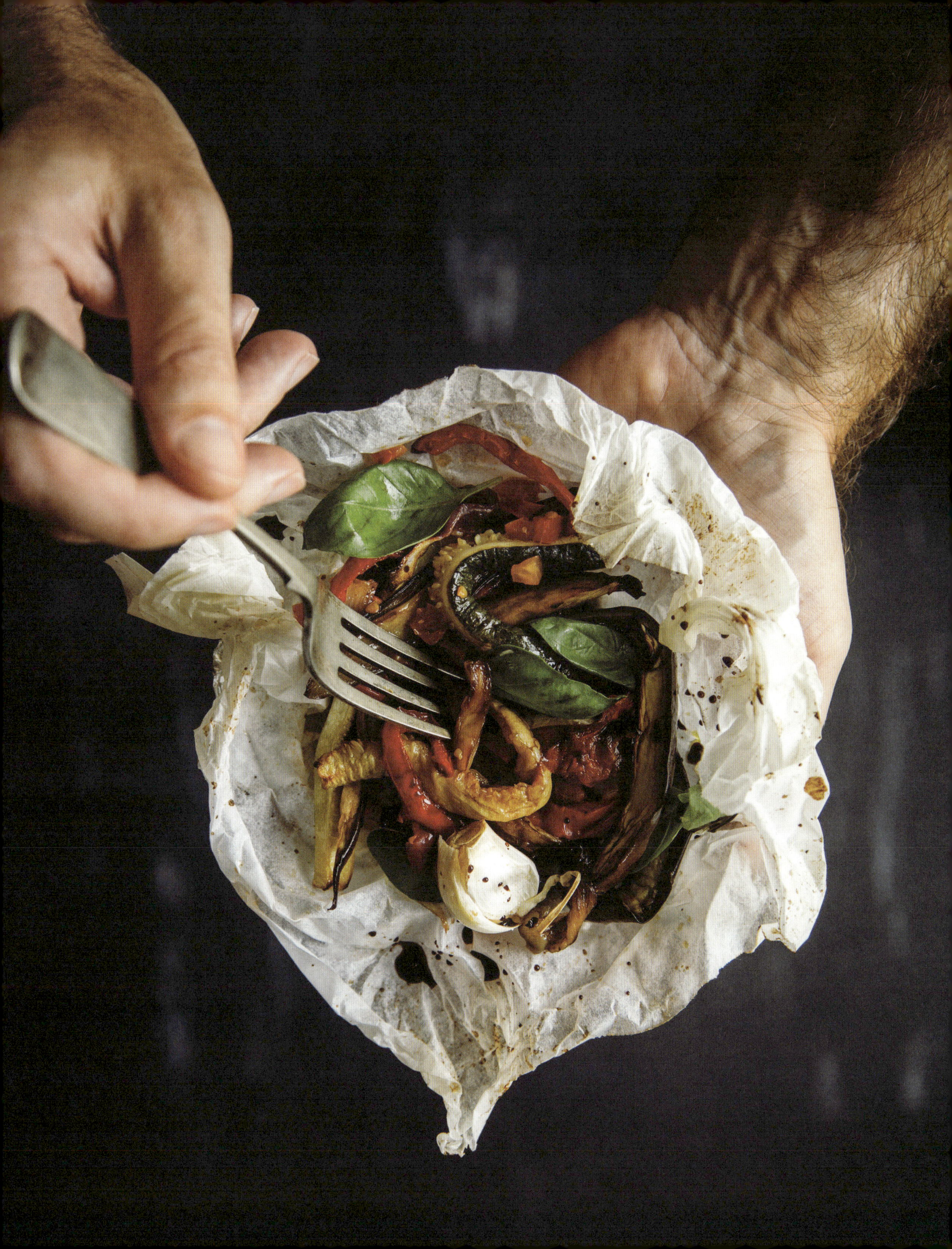

YEASTED GRILLED FLATBREAD

MAKES 4

300 g (2 cups) strong flour
1 teaspoon sea salt flakes
1½ teaspoons active dried yeast
3 teaspoons butter, softened
about 150 ml warm water

Place the flour, salt and yeast in a large mixing bowl. Add the butter and two-thirds of the water and mix by hand until the mixture comes together. Mix in enough of the remaining water for a dough to form.

Tip onto a lightly floured surface and knead the dough for 7–8 minutes until smooth and silky. Return the dough to the mixing bowl, cover with a clean damp dish towel and set aside in a warm place for about 1 hour, until the dough has doubled in size.

Preheat a barbecue hotplate to medium high and lightly grease with oil.

Flour your surface again. Tip the dough onto the surface and knock back to get the air out. Divide the dough into six portions and roll into balls. Roll out into ovals about 5 mm thick. Transfer to a lightly-oiled baking tray and set aside for 10–15 minutes.

Place the flatbreads on the hotplate and cook for about 3–4 minutes on each side until browned and blistered. Serve immediately.

UNLEAVENED GRILLED FLATBREAD

MAKES 4

300 g (2 cups) strong flour, plus extra if needed
¼ teaspoon ground cumin
¼ teaspoon ground coriander
¾ teaspoon sea salt flakes
50 g butter, melted
185 ml (¾ cups) warm milk

In a large bowl, combine the flour, cumin, coriander, salt, butter and milk until a dough forms.

Tip onto a lightly floured surface and knead the dough for a few minutes until smooth. If the dough is too sticky, add a little extra flour. Wrap with plastic wrap and rest at room temperature for 30 minutes.

Preheat a barbecue hotplate to medium high and lightly grease with oil.

Flour your surface again. Divide the dough into four portions and roll into balls. Roll out into rounds about 5 mm thick.

Place the flatbreads on the hotplate and cook for about 1 minute on each side, turning when the dough begins to bubble. Serve immediately.

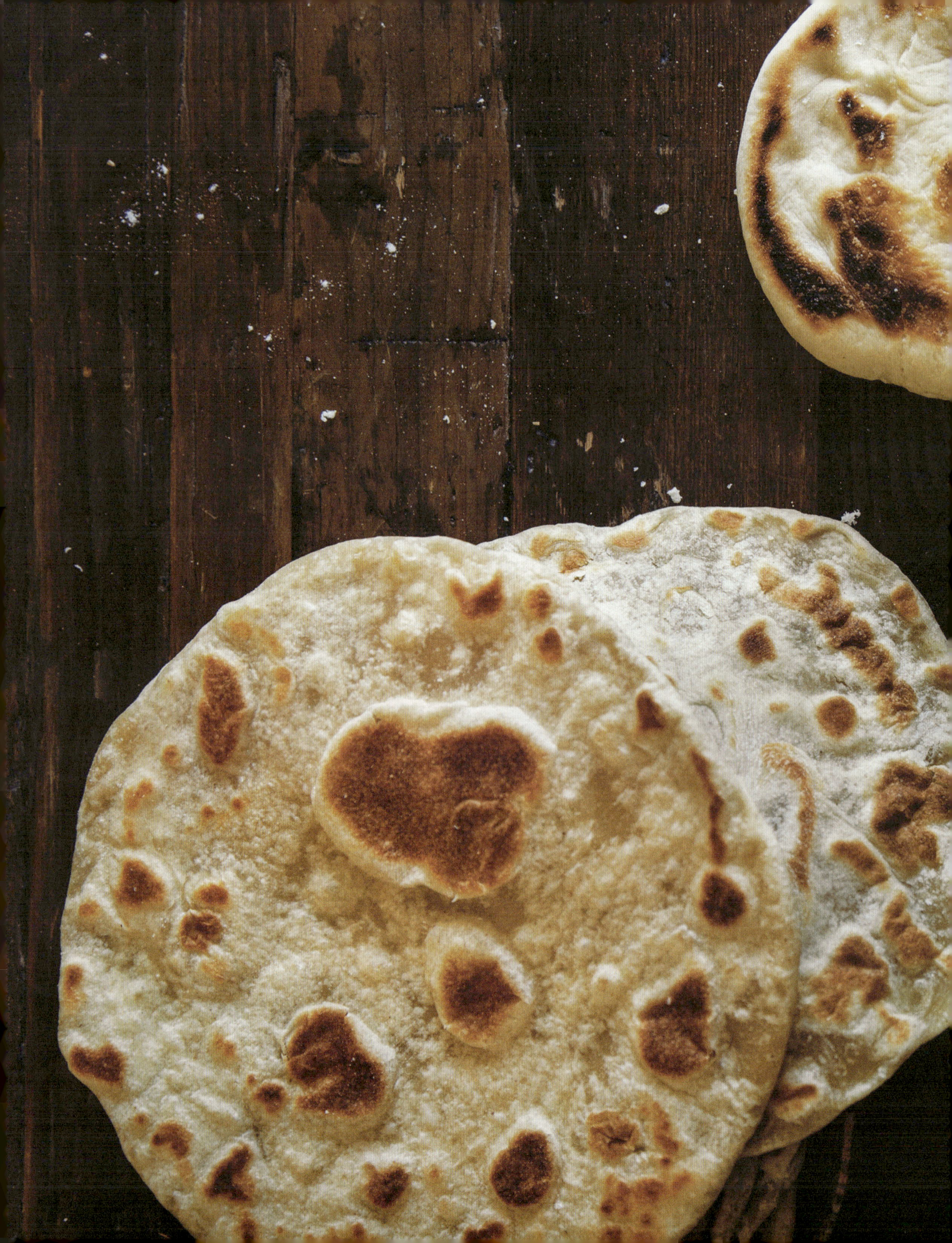

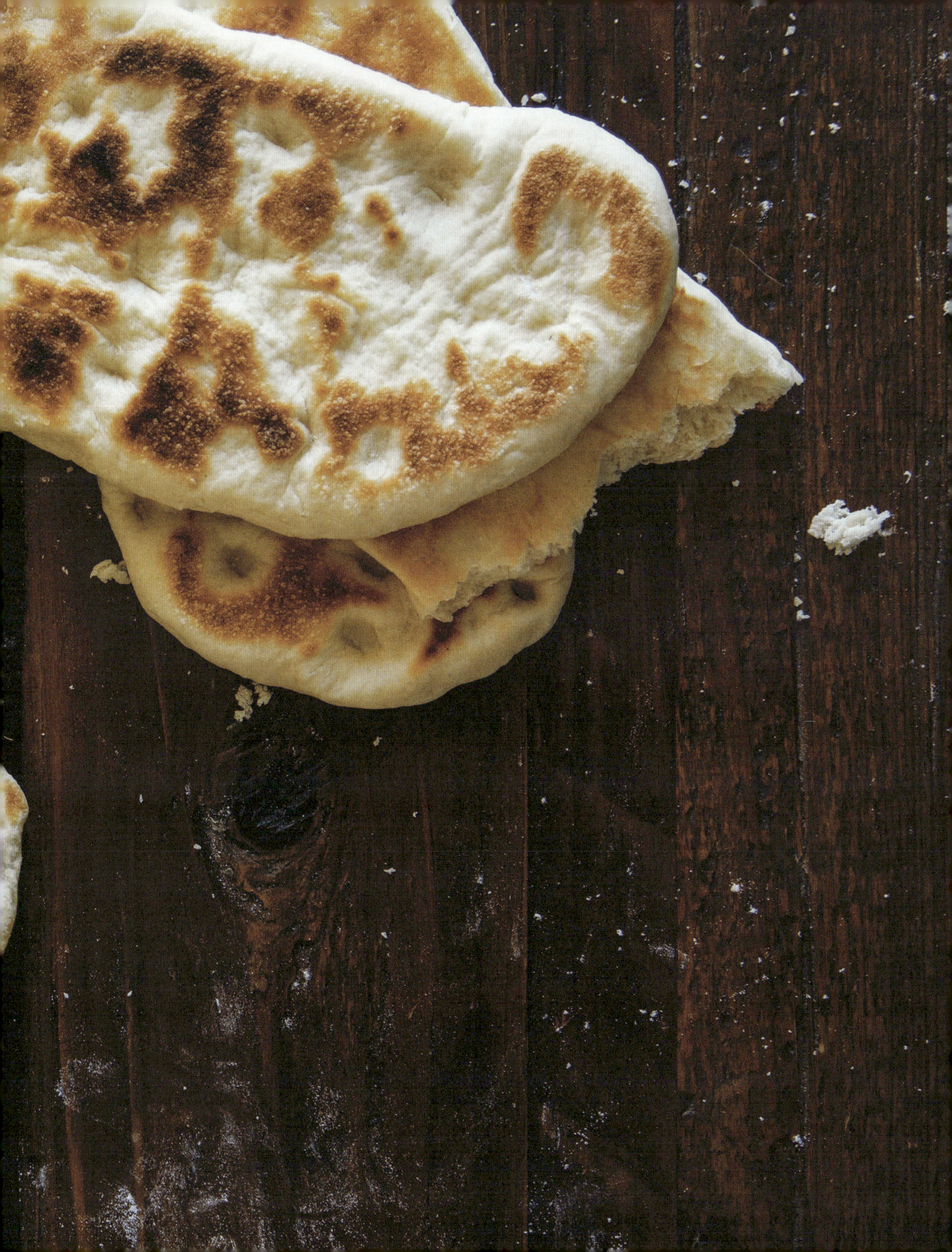

Barbecued Potato Wedges with Lime Yoghurt

SERVES 4 AS A SIDE

4 large floury potatoes, cut into wedges about 3 cm thick
80 ml (⅓ cup) olive oil

SEASONING
1 teaspoon sweet paprika
1 teaspoon of ancho chilli powder
1 teaspoon sea salt flakes
½ teaspoon soft brown sugar

LIME YOGHURT
185 g (¾ cup) Greek yoghurt
zest of ½ lime
2 teaspoons chopped coriander leaves

Preheat a barbecue grill to medium high and lightly grease with oil.

To make the seasoning, combine the paprika, chilli, salt and sugar in a small bowl.

Bring a large saucepan of salted water to the boil over high heat. Boil the potato wedges for 5 minutes. Drain well.

To make the lime yoghurt, mix the yoghurt, lime zest and coriander in a small bowl.

Brush the wedges with olive oil and place on the grill. Cook for 5–6 minutes on each side or until browned and crispy on the outside and tender inside.

Transfer the potatoes to a large bowl. Sprinkle with the spice mixture and toss to coat. Serve immediately with lime yoghurt alongside for dipping.

HERBY NEW POTATO SALAD

SERVES 4 AS A SIDE

500 g small red new potatoes
½ teaspoon dijon mustard
½ teaspoon sea salt flakes
¼ teaspoon freshly ground black pepper
60 ml (¼ cup) olive oil
1 small red onion, very finely diced
2 tablespoons chopped chives
1 tablespoon chopped flat-leaf parsley

Place the potatoes in a medium-sized saucepan over high heat and cover with cold water. Bring to the boil, then reduce heat to medium–low and simmer for 10–15 minutes until tender when tested with a skewer (be careful not to overcook as the skins may split and the potatoes will become waterlogged). Drain and set aside to cool slightly.

In a small bowl, combine the mustard, salt, pepper and olive oil.

Cut the potatoes into bite-sized pieces and place in a medium-sized bowl along with the onion. Pour the dressing over while the potatoes are still hot, and toss to combine.

Allow to cool. Stir the chives and parsley through before serving.

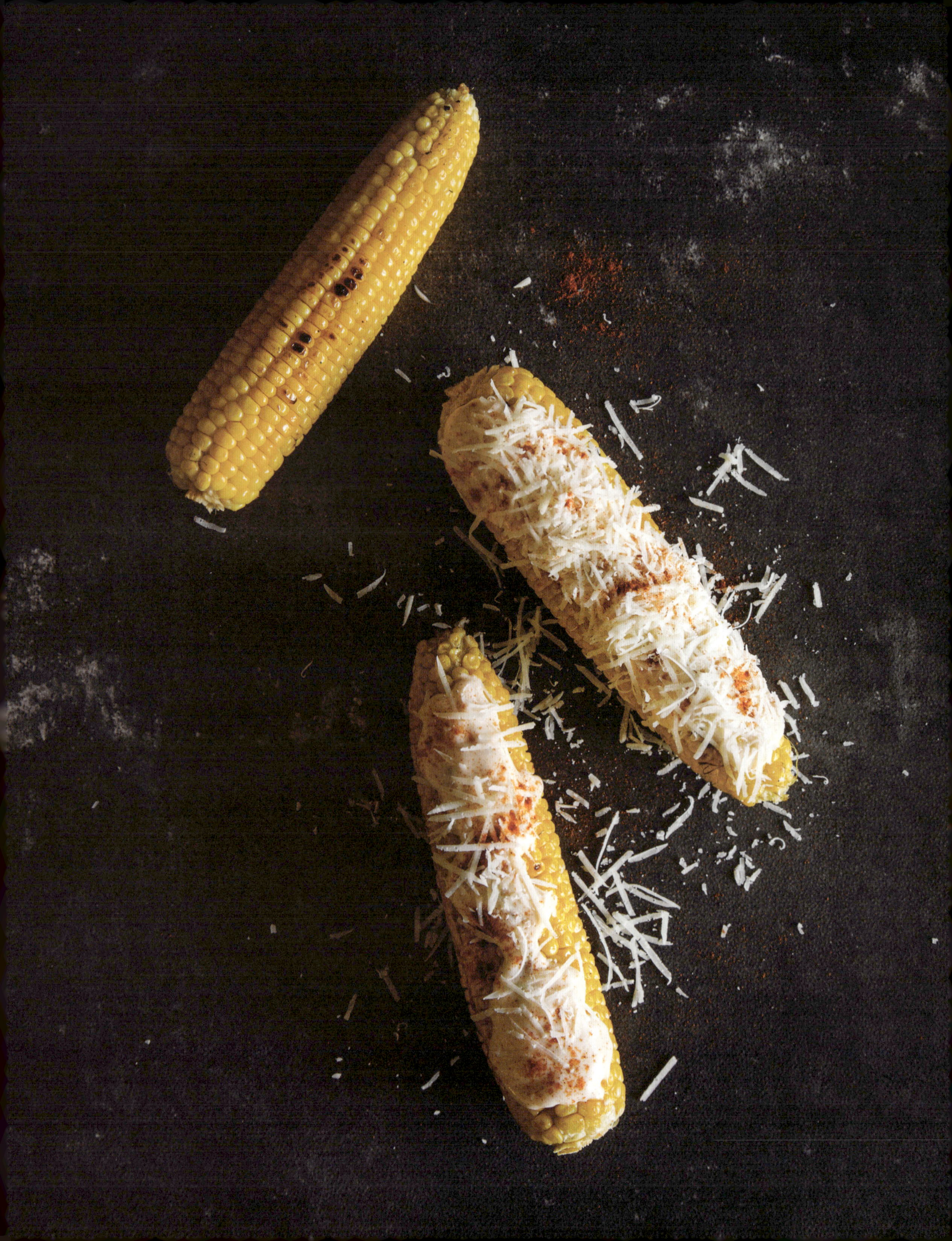

MEXICAN CORN ON THE COB

SERVES 4 AS A SIDE

4 corn cobs, husks removed
smoked paprika, for sprinkling
¼ cup finely grated manchego or parmesan cheese
1 lime, quartered, to serve

CHIPOTLE MAYO

juice of 1 lime
1 tablespoon chipotle sauce
125 g (½ cup) good-quality whole egg mayonnaise

Heat a barbecue grill to high and lightly grease with oil.

Blanch the corn in a large saucepan of boiling water for 1 minute, then drain.

To make the chipotle mayo, combine the ingredients in a small bowl, stirring to combine well.

Brush or spray the corn with olive oil and cook on the grill, turning occasionally, for about 10 minutes or until charred. Transfer to a platter.

Spread a small spoonful of chipotle mayo over each cob. Sprinkle with smoked paprika and cheese.

Serve with any remaining chipotle mayonnaise and with lime wedges for squeezing.

APPLE & CABBAGE SLAW

SERVES 4 AS A SIDE

¼ small red cabbage, finely shredded
¼ small green cabbage, finely shredded
2 small granny smith apples, cut into matchsticks
4 spring onions, finely sliced
1 cup coriander leaves, roughly chopped

DRESSING
2 tablespoons lime juice
1 tablespoon cider vinegar
2 teaspoons dijon mustard
½ teaspoon salt
2 tablespoons olive oil

Combine the cabbage, apple, spring onions and coriander in a large bowl.

To make the dressing, combine the lime juice, vinegar, mustard, salt and olive oil in a small bowl.

Pour the dressing over the salad and toss to combine well.

CHARGRILLED WITLOF

SERVES 4 AS A SIDE

4 large witlof, halved lengthways
olive oil, for drizzling
juice of 1 lemon
1 tablespoon finely chopped flat-leaf parsley

Preheat a barbecue grill to high and lightly grease with oil.

Brush the witlof halves with oil and season lightly with salt and freshly ground black pepper.

Place the cut-side down for 2–3 minutes, then turn and cook on the other side for another 2 minutes.

To serve, drizzle with a little extra olive oil and the lemon juice, and sprinkle with parsley.

FRESH CORN, BACON, KALE & JALAPENO SALAD

SERVES 4

4 slices middle bacon, rind removed
2 corn cobs, husks and silks removed
olive oil, for brushing
6–8 curly kale leaves, stems removed and leaves shredded
250 g mixed cherry tomatoes, halved
2 avocados, cut into thick slices
4 spring onions, finely chopped
½ jalapeño chilli, deseeded and thinly sliced
toasted pepitas, to serve

TANGY LIME DRESSING

1 large egg yolk
80 ml (⅓ cup) lime juice
30 g (1 cup) coriander leaves with some chopped stalk
2 teaspoons honey
½ jalapeño chilli, deseeded and thinly sliced
125 ml (½ cup) olive oil
60 ml (¼ cup) vegetable oil

Cook the bacon in a non-stick frying pan over medium–high heat for 6–8 minutes, turning occasionally until browned and crisp. Transfer to a chopping board and cut into pieces.

Meanwhile, preheat a barbecue grill to medium.

Brush the corn with a little oil and cook on all sides until just charred and the kernels are tender. Remove, cool and cut off the kernels.

Combine the kale, tomato, avocado, corn, spring onion and chilli in a large salad bowl.

For the dressing, combine the egg yolk, lime juice, coriander, honey, chilli and a pinch of salt in a small food processor and blend until the coriander is finely chopped. Combine the oils in a jug. While the motor is running, pour in the oils in a slow steady stream until the mixture has thickened. Season with pepper. If the dressing is too thick, just add a small amount of warm water.

Lightly toss the salad ingredients with the dressing. Scatter the bacon pieces over and top with toasted pepitas.

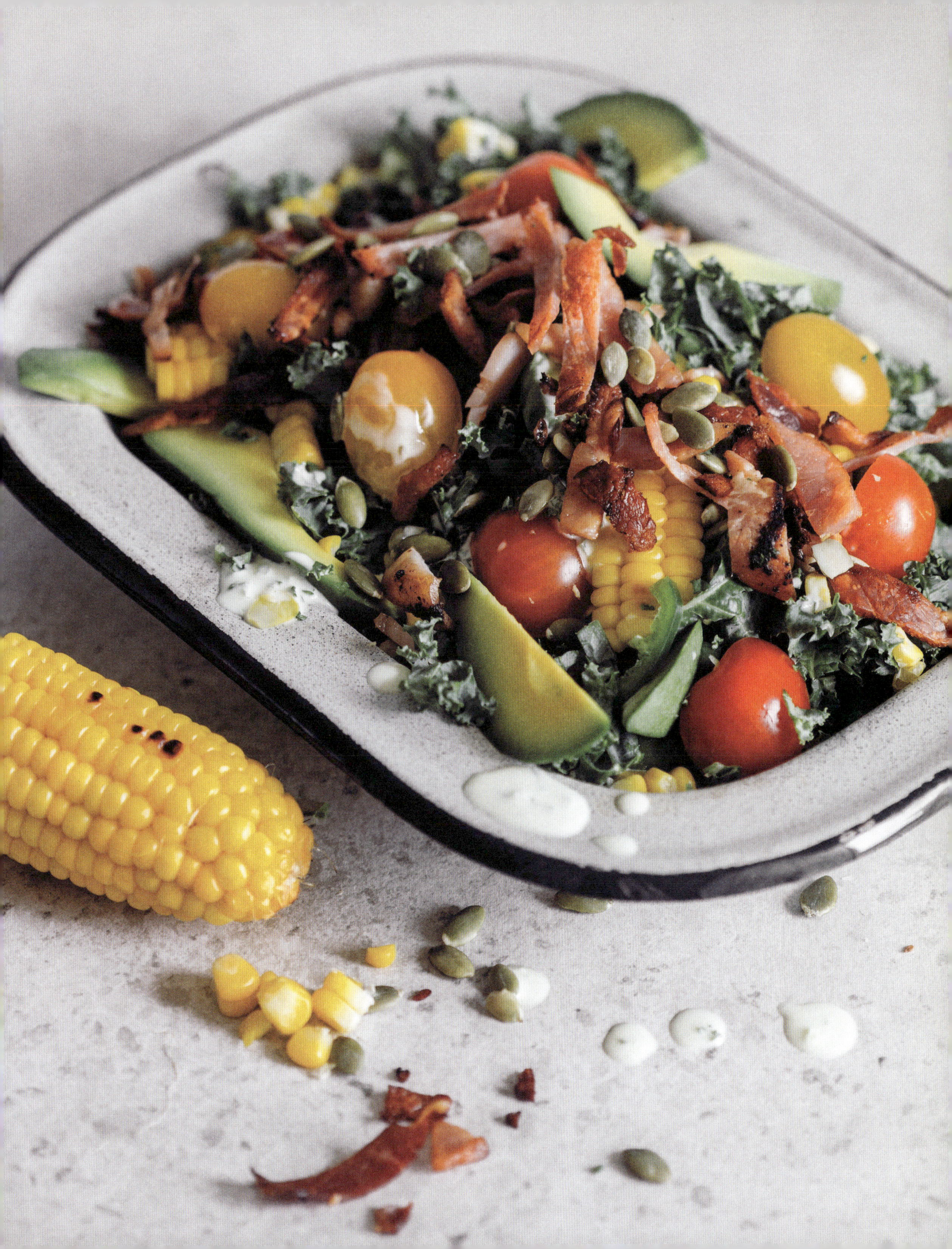

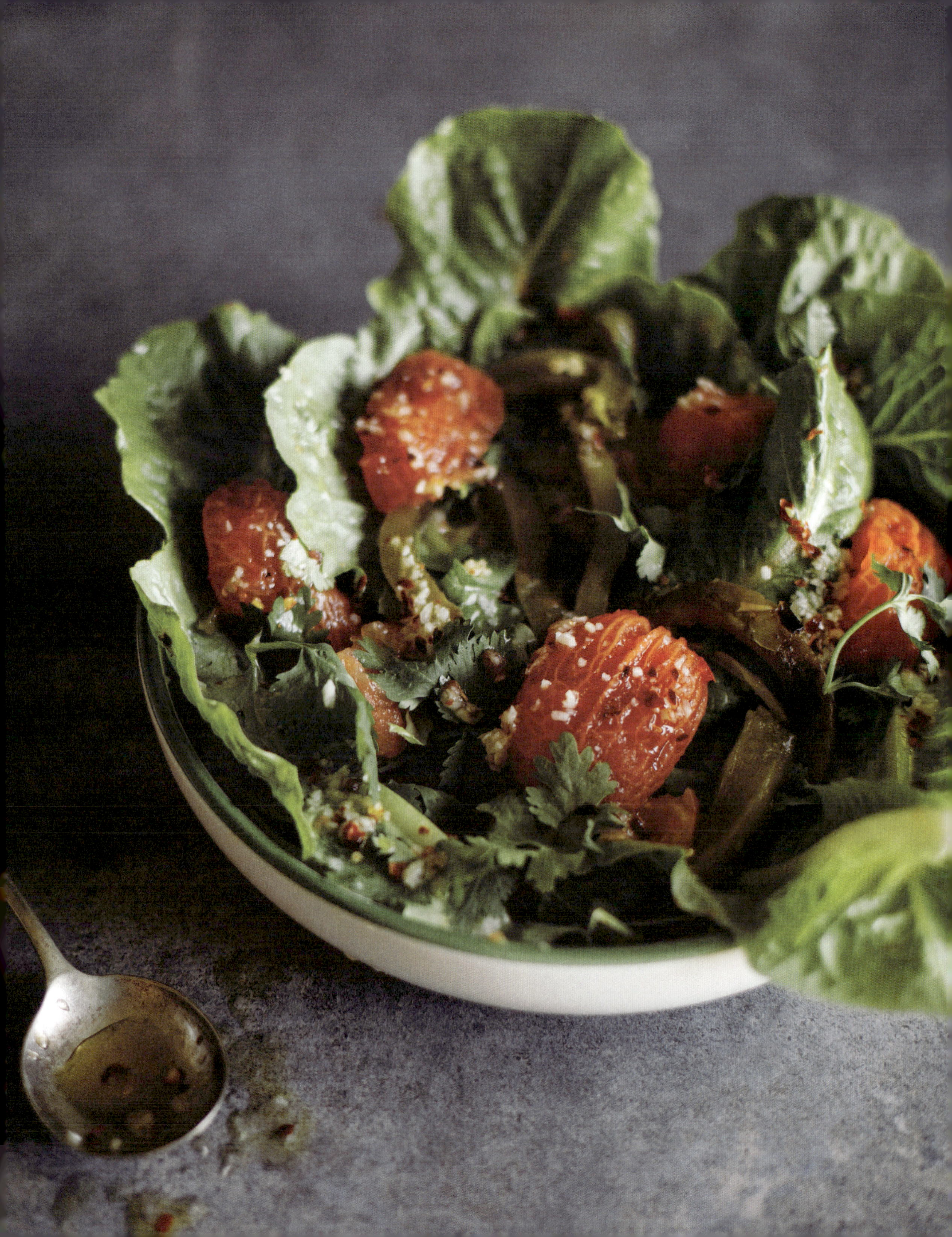

PORTUGUESE SALAD

SERVES 6 AS A SIDE

3 green capsicums
6 roma (plum) tomatoes
3 garlic cloves, unpeeled
pinch of sea salt flakes
pinch of dried chilli flakes
60 ml (¼ cup) extra-virgin olive oil
2 tablespoons sherry vinegar
1 baby cos lettuce, leaves separated
½ cup coriander leaves

Preheat a barbecue grill to high and lightly grease with oil.

Place the capsicums, tomatoes and garlic cloves on the grill to cook, turning occasionally with tongs, until the skins are charred and blistered all over. Transfer to a bowl, cover with plastic wrap and set aside to cool.

Peel the skins from the capsicums, tomatoes and garlic. Remove and discard the capsicum seeds and chop tomatoes and capsicums roughly.

Pound the garlic, salt and chilli flakes into a paste using a mortar and pestle. Combine with the olive oil and sherry vinegar to make a dressing.

Combine the capsicum, tomato, lettuce and coriander in a salad bowl. Pour the dressing over and toss to combine.

GRILLED EGGPLANT WITH SAGE OIL

SERVES 4–6 AS A SIDE

- 12 sage leaves, finely chopped, plus extra to garnish
- 1 teaspoon sea salt flakes
- 100 ml olive oil
- 2 eggplants, sliced lengthways

Combine the sage leaves, salt and olive oil in a small bowl. Brush the slices of eggplant with the sage oil. Allow to stand for 1 hour.

Preheat a barbecue grill to medium and lightly grease with oil.

Grill the eggplant slices for 2–3 minutes on each side until soft, and grill marks appear. Garnish with sage leaves to serve.

Note: Look for eggplants that have glossy skins and fresh green stems.

ROASTED CHICKPEA & GARLIC HOMMUS

SERVES 6 AS A SIDE

200 g dry chickpeas
4 garlic cloves, unpeeled
2 tablespoons olive oil
1 teaspoon sea salt flakes
2 tablespoons lemon juice
½ teaspoon ground cumin
135 g (½ cup) tahini
za'atar (see page 125, but make without the olive oil and lemon juice), to garnish
extra-virgin olive oil, for drizzling

Soak the chickpeas overnight in 1 litre cold water. Rinse and drain well. Transfer the chickpeas to a large saucepan and cover with 1.5 litres (6 cups) water. Simmer gently, covered, for about 1½ hours or until very tender. Drain, reserving the cooking liquid. Rinse the chickpeas in water and drain again.

Preheat the oven to 180°C.

In a medium-sized bowl, combine the chickpeas, garlic cloves and olive oil. Spread onto a baking tray lined with baking paper and bake for 20 minutes or until the chickpeas start to colour. Remove from the oven and set aside to cool a little.

When cool enough to handle, squeeze the garlic from the skins. Place the garlic and chickpeas in a food processor along with the salt, lemon juice, cumin, tahini and 170 ml (⅔ cup) of the reserved chickpea cooking liquid.

Pulse for a few minutes, or until creamy. Adjust the thickness if required by adding a little warm water. The hommus will thicken on standing. Transfer to a small serving bowl and sprinkle with za'atar and drizzle with extra-virgin olive oil.

Grilled Cauliflower & Sweet Potato Salad with Tahini-Yoghurt Dressing

SERVES 4 AS A SIDE

1 cauliflower, cut into florets

500 g sweet potato, peeled, cut into 2 cm pieces

1 large red onion, cut into thin wedges

2 garlic cloves, crushed

2 cm piece ginger, grated

1 long red chilli, finely chopped

80 ml (⅓ cup) extra-virgin olive oil

400 g tinned chickpeas, rinsed and drained

⅔ cup coriander leaves, chopped

SPICE MIX

2 teaspoons ground cumin

2 teaspoons ground coriander

1 teaspoon ground cinnamon

½ teaspoon ground allspice

TAHINI-YOGHURT DRESSING

125 g (½ cup) Greek-style yoghurt

1 tablespoon tahini

1 garlic clove, crushed

1 tablespoon lemon juice

Preheat a barbecue hotplate to medium and lightly grease with oil.

To make the spice mix, combine the ingredients in a small bowl.

In a large bowl, combine the cauliflower, sweet potato, onion, garlic, ginger, chilli and olive oil.

Cook the vegetable mix on the hotplate, turning regularly, for 8–10 minutes or until the sweet potato is cooked through. Return to the mixing bowl and set aside to cool.

To make the dressing, combine the ingredients in a bowl.

Add the chickpeas to the vegetables and then sprinkle the spice mix and coriander over the top. Stir through to combine well.

Pour the dressing over the salad just before serving and toss well to coat.

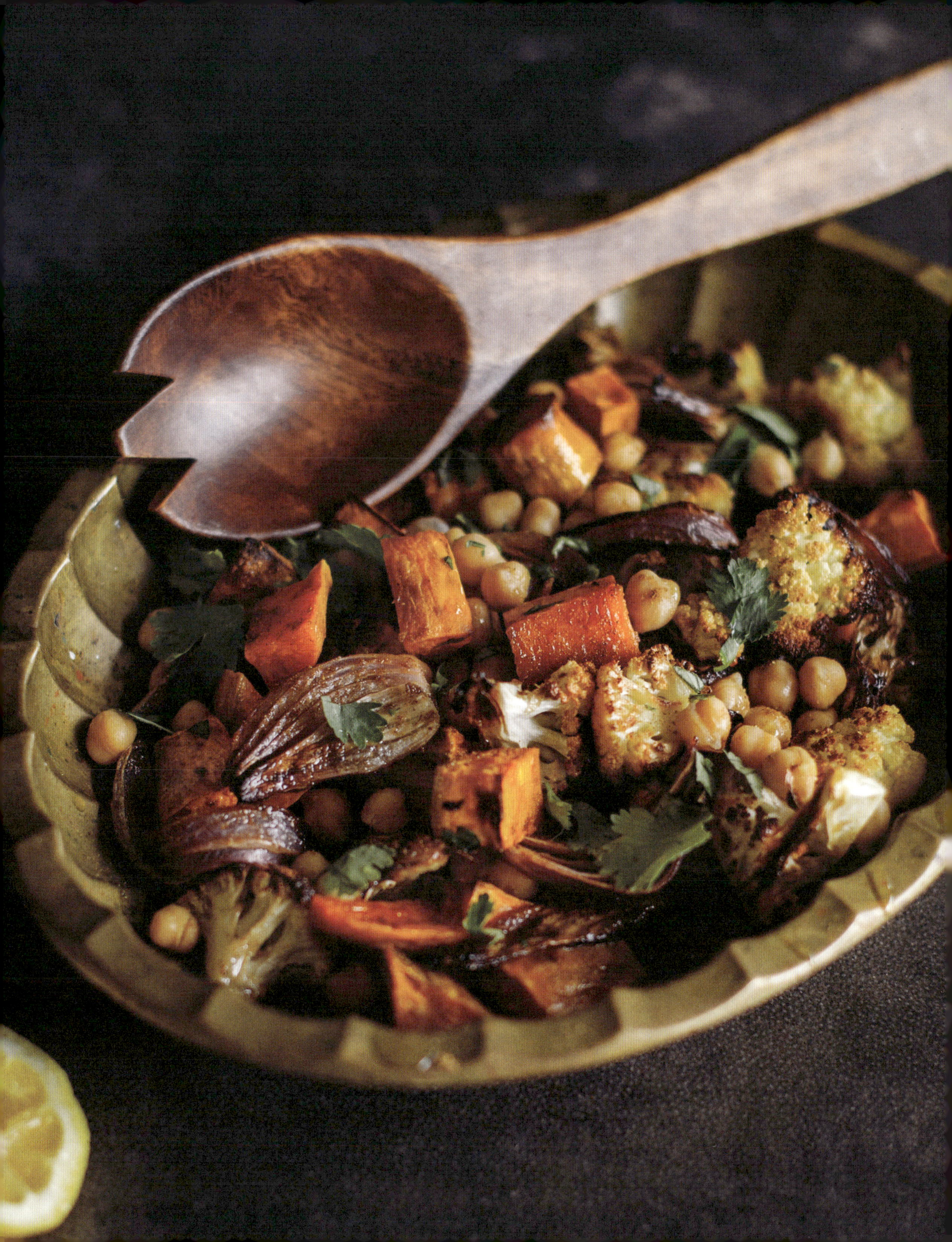

BARBECUED BAKED POTATOES SERVES 4

4 whole washed potatoes or small sweet potatoes

Preheat a hooded barbecue grill to medium and grease with oil.

Poke a few deep holes in the potatoes with a metal skewer. Wrap each potato in two layers of foil, ensuring they are well covered.

Place the potatoes on the grill and cover. Cook for 30 minutes, then turn and cook for another 20–30 minutes longer, until the flesh is tender (test by inserting a metal skewer).

Remove the foil from the potato and cook, turning occasionally, for 10 minutes, until browned all over.

Serve with any of the toppings opposite.

AVOCADO, FETA & DUKKAH

1 tablespoon almonds
1 tablespoon pistachio nuts
1 tablespoon pine nuts
2 teaspoons coriander seeds
2 teaspoons cumin seeds
1 tablespoon sesame seeds
½ teaspoon sea salt flakes
pinch of cinnamon
pinch of nutmeg
Barbecued baked potatoes
  (see recipe left)
100 g feta cheese, crumbled
1 avocado, mashed roughly

Toast the almonds and pistachios in a large frying pan over medium-high heat, stirring, for 5 minutes until just starting to colour and become fragrant. Set aside and add the pine nuts and coriander seeds to the hot pan. Toast and stir for a minute, and then add the cumin and sesame seeds. Continue to toast, stirring, until golden brown.

Using a mortar and pestle, pound the nuts, toasted spices, salt, cinnamon and nutmeg until coarsely ground.

Split the tops of the baked potatoes and fill with feta and avocado and sprinkle with dukkah.

CHEESE & SPRING ONION COLESLAW

75 g (1 cup) finely sliced red cabbage
75 g (1 cup) finely sliced green cabbage
1 carrot, grated
1 tablespoon white vinegar
1 teaspoon caster sugar
1 teaspoon sea salt flakes
3 tablespoons whole egg mayonnaise
4 spring onions, finely chopped
120 g aged cheddar cheese, grated

In a medium-sized mixing bowl, combine the cabbage and carrot. Sprinkle with the vinegar, sugar and salt and toss to combine well. Set aside for 1 hour.

The cabbage will release liquid, so drain and squeeze out any excess moisture. Place the drained cabbage mixture into a clean mixing bowl along with the mayonnaise and spring onions and stir to combine.

Split the tops of the potatoes and fill with cheddar cheese. Place the potatoes back on the grill, close the hood and cook for 4–5 minutes until the cheese has melted. Top with coleslaw to serve.

SMOKED TROUT & HORSE-RADISH CRÈME

200 g crème fraiche
2 teaspoons finely grated horseradish
2 tablespoons chopped chives
200 g smoked trout, flaked into small chunks
Barbecued baked sweet potatoes
  (see recipe left)
¼ red onion, finely chopped
lemon wedges to serve

In a medium-sized bowl, combine the crème fraiche, horseradish and chives. Gently stir in the smoked trout.

Split the tops of the sweet potatoes and fill with smoked trout mixture. Add a teaspoon of red onion to the top of each and serve with lemon wedges for squeezing.

SIDES & SALADS

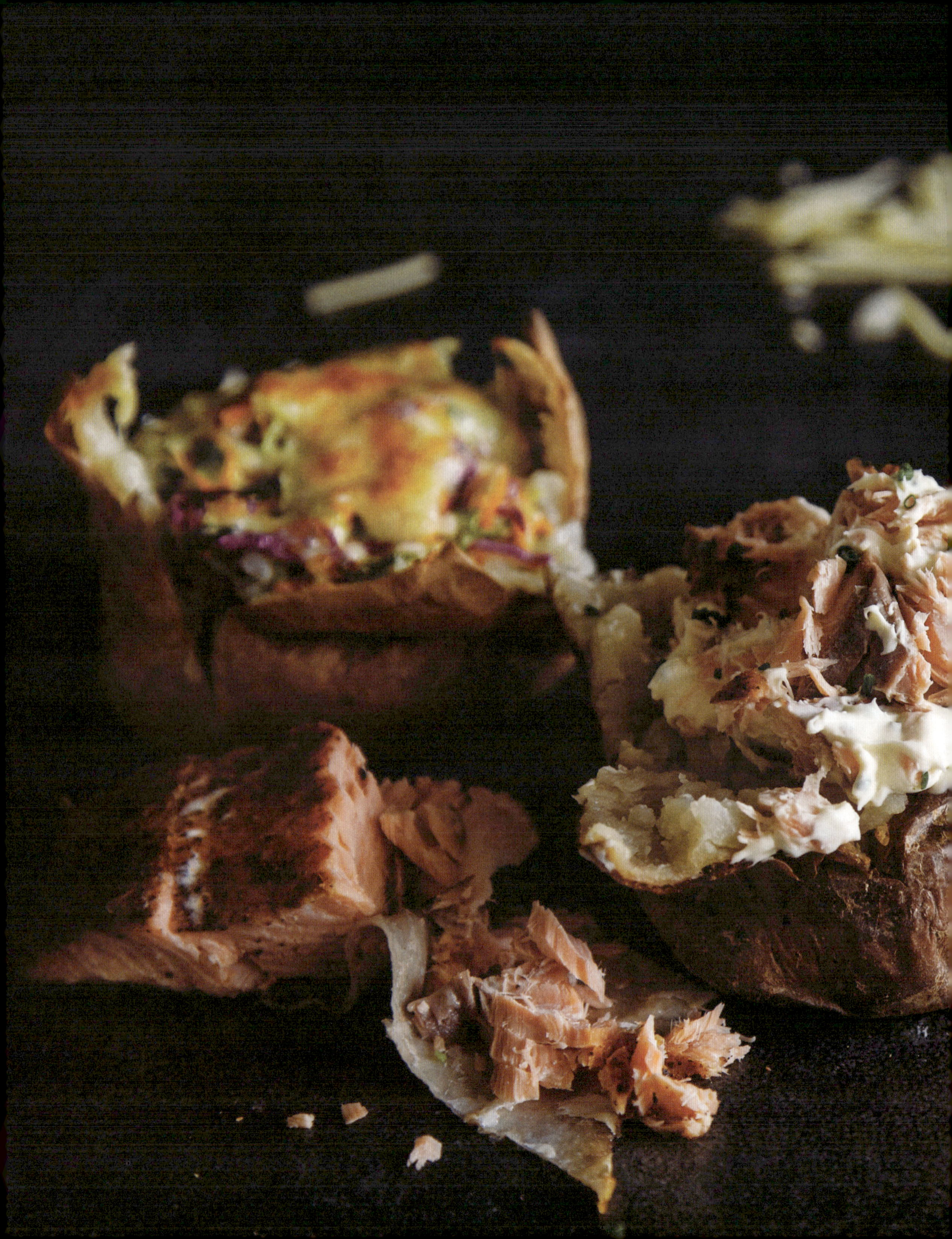

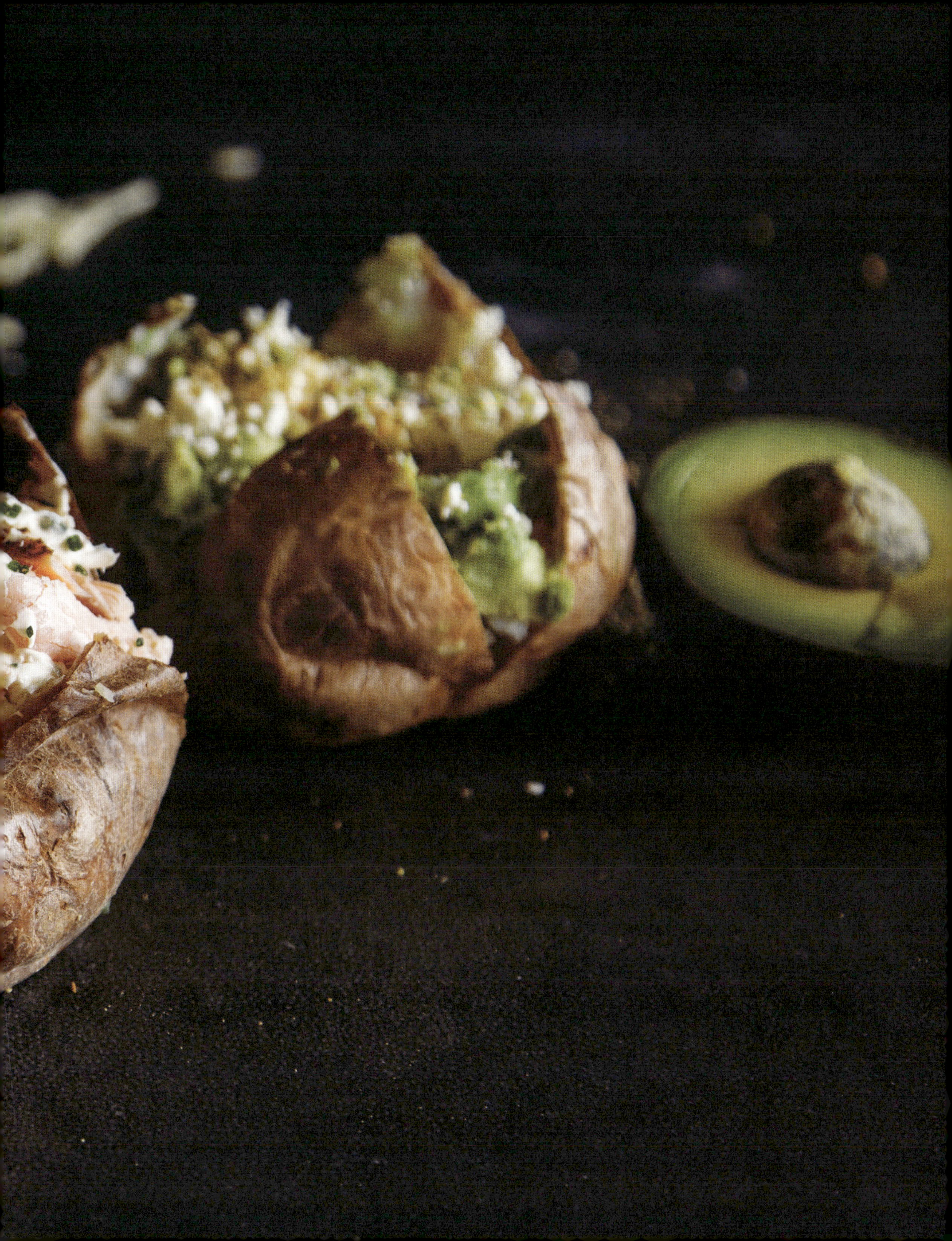

GERMAN POTATO SALAD

SERVES 6 AS A SIDE

3 eggs
1 teaspoon olive oil
200 g bacon, cut into batons
1 kg new potatoes
3 chicken stock cubes
½ red onion, thinly sliced
15 cornichons, sliced lengthways
1 small bunch flat-leaf parsley, chopped
1 small bunch chives, chopped

DRESSING
125 ml (½ cup) olive oil
3 tablespoons white wine vinegar
2 tablespoons dijon mustard
pinch of sugar

In a small bowl, whisk together the ingredients for the dressing, season with salt and black pepper and set aside.

Place the eggs in a small saucepan, cover with cold water and bring to the boil over high heat. Reduce to a rolling simmer and continue cooking for 6 minutes. Remove from the heat and place the eggs directly into iced water. Once cool, peel and cut in half.

Heat the olive oil in a frying pan over high heat and add the bacon. Cook until crisp, then remove with a slotted spoon and set aside to drain on paper towel.

Place the potatoes in a large saucepan, cover with water and bring to the boil. Add the stock cubes and cook for about 15 minutes, or until potatoes are tender. Drain, then halve or quarter the potatoes depending on their size. Transfer to a large bowl and allow to cool for a few minutes. Add the red onion, bacon, cornichons, herbs and the dressing. Toss to combine until everything is evenly coated in the dressing, then add the eggs and gently combine. Serve warm.

Note: The potatoes should be warm when tossed with the other ingredients, so best prepare everything else first.

CUCUMBER SALAD

SERVES 4–6 AS A SIDE

2 long cucumbers
1 teaspoon table salt
½ red onion, thinly sliced
1 small bunch dill, chopped

DRESSING
3 tablespoons white vinegar
1 pinch of sugar
1 teaspoon celery salt
200 g sour cream

Peel one of the cucumbers, then slice both cucumbers as thinly as possible.

Place the cucumbers in a bowl, then add the salt and toss to combine. Set aside for 30–60 minutes, then drain away the excess liquid, lightly squeezing the cucumber to release excess moisture. Transfer to a clean bowl, add the red onion and toss to combine.

To make the dressing, mix the vinegar, sugar, celery salt and sour cream in a small bowl until well combined. Season with black pepper.

Pour the dressing over the cucumber and onion and sprinkle with the chopped dill.

Toss to combine until the ingredients are evenly coasted, then season to taste and serve immediately.

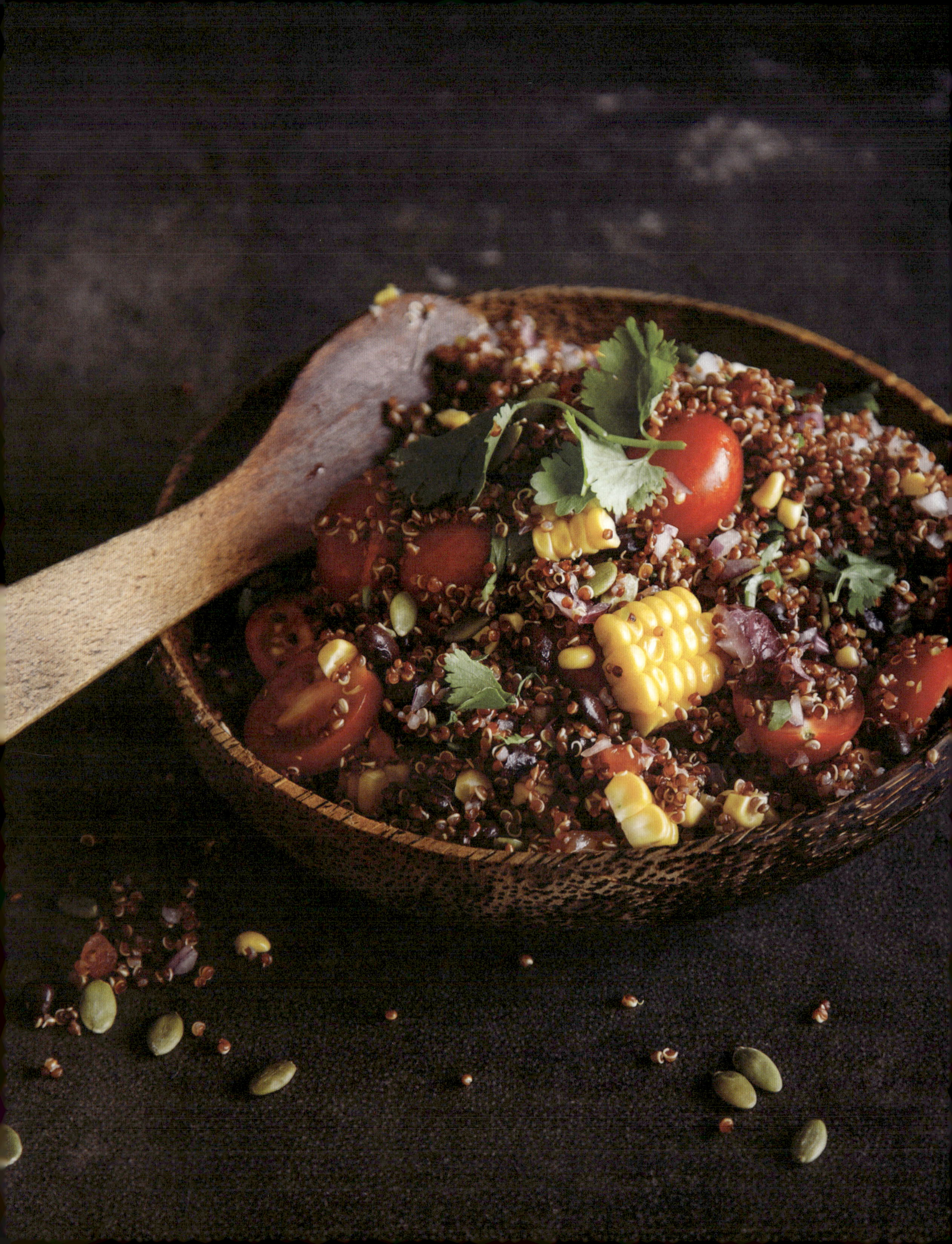

MEXICAN QUINOA SALAD

SERVES 6 AS A SIDE

2 corn cobs, husks removed

300 g (1½ cups) red quinoa, rinsed thoroughly

250 g grape tomatoes, halved

1 red capsicum, diced

1 red onion, finely diced

1 jalapeño chilli, very finely diced

400 g tinned black beans, rinsed and drained

2 cups coriander leaves, finely chopped

30 g (¼ cup) pepitas (pumpkin seeds)

DRESSING

2 tablespoons olive oil

juice of 2 limes

½ teaspoon sea salt flakes

1 teaspoon smoked paprika

½ teaspoon ground cumin

Heat a barbecue grill to high and lightly grease with oil.

Blanch the corn in a large pot of boiling water for 1 minute, then drain. Brush or spray the corn with olive oil and cook on the grill, turning occasionally, for about 10 minutes or until charred. Set aside to cool then cut the kernels off the cobs.

Bring 750 ml of water to boil in a medium saucepan over high heat. Add the quinoa, cover and simmer for about 15 minutes or until all the moisture is absorbed. Remove from the heat and keep covered.

To make the dressing, combine the ingredients in a bowl and whisk well.

To assemble the salad, mix the quinoa, corn, tomatoes, capsicum, onion, chilli and beans in a large bowl. Pour the dressing over, add the coriander and toss to combine. Sprinkle with the pepitas.

Serve at room temperature.

TURKISH ROASTED TOMATO SALAD

SERVES 4–6 AS A SIDE

6 medium roma (plum) tomatoes
4 large long red sweet peppers (such as bullhorn or cubanelle)
2 red capsicums, finely chopped
1 bunch flat-leaf parsley, leaves finely chopped
1 red onion, coarsely chopped

DRESSING
2 garlic cloves, finely chopped
½ teaspoon chilli flakes
1 teaspoon sweet paprika
1 teaspoon sea salt flakes
1 tablespoon lemon juice
60 ml (¼ cup) extra-virgin olive oil
1 tablespoon pomegranate molasses

Preheat a barbecue grill to medium–high and lightly grease with oil.

Cook the tomatoes and sweet peppers over the grill, turning occasionally, for 6–8 minutes until the skins are blackened and blistering. Seal in a plastic container or bag and set aside to cool. Remove and discard the skins, stems and seeds. (Don't rinse as it will wash away the delicious charred flavour.)

Finely chop the tomato and pepper flesh and transfer to a large mixing bowl. Add the capsicum, parsley and onion and mix to combine.

To make the dressing, combine the ingredients in a small bowl. Stir well to blend.

Pour the dressing over the salad and toss well. Cover and refrigerate for 1 hour to allow the flavours to develop.

Serve at room temperature.

HOMEMADE TOMATO KETCHUP

MAKES 1.25 LITRES

3 kg tomatoes, roughly chopped
2 granny smith apples, cored and roughly chopped
1 onion, roughly chopped
1 cinnamon stick
2 garlic cloves, crushed
1 teaspoon freshly ground black pepper
1 teaspoon ground allspice
600 g raw caster sugar
2 tablespoons sea salt flakes
400 ml apple cider vinegar

Place all the ingredients in a large saucepan over low heat. Simmer for 2 hours, uncovered, stirring frequently or until the sauce reduces and thickens to a saucy consistency.

Strain the mixture through a fine-meshed sieve into a large bowl, pressing down to extract the liquid. Discard solids.

Pour the hot mixture into sterilised bottles and seal. Store in a cool, dark place until ready to use. Once opened, the sauce will keep for up to 1 month in the refrigerator.

GRILLED CABBAGE SALAD

SERVES 4 AS A SIDE

45 g (¼ cup) palm sugar
60 ml (¼ cup) lime juice
2 tablespoons fish sauce
2 garlic cloves, crushed
½ green cabbage, cut into thin wedges
¼ red cabbage, cut into thin wedges
2 tablespoons peanut oil
2 red Asian shallots, finely diced
1 long red chili, thinly sliced

Preheat a barbecue hotplate to medium and lightly grease with oil.

Combine the palm sugar, lime juice, fish sauce and garlic in a small saucepan over low heat. Simmer for 3–4 minutes until the sugar has dissolved and the mixture has reduced by a third. Remove from the heat.

Brush the cabbage wedges with the peanut oil and cook on the hotplate for 6–8 minutes on each side, allowing the edges to blacken slightly.

Transfer to a chopping board and remove the cores from the cabbage. Place the cabbage wedges in a serving bowl and pour the dressing over.

Garnish with the shallots and chilli.

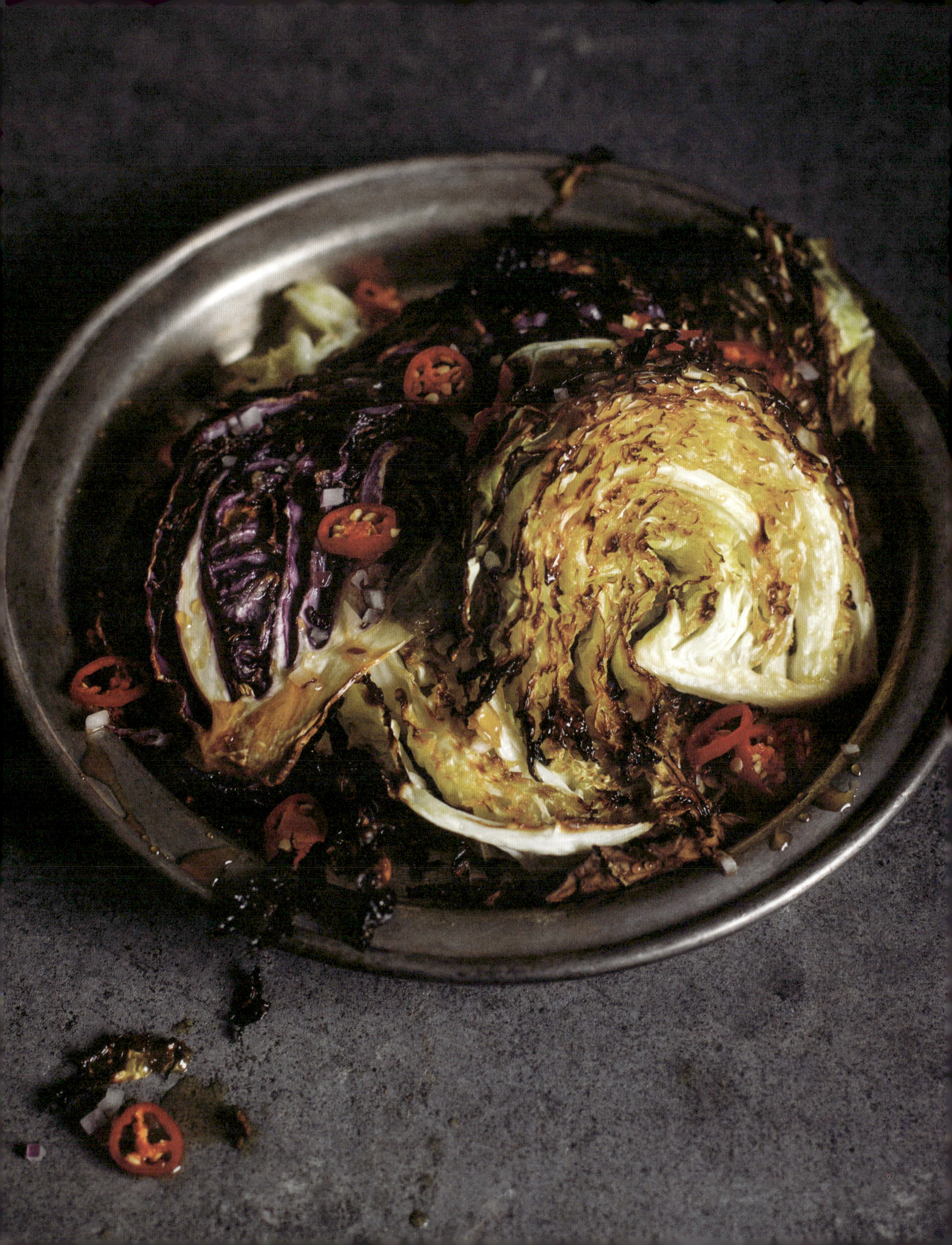

WHITE BEAN SALAD WITH FRESH HERBS

SERVES 4–6

300 g (1½ cups) dried haricot, navy or cannellini beans
3 flat-leaf parsley sprigs
2 thyme sprigs
1 bay leaf
2 garlic cloves, unpeeled
2 tablespoons white wine vinegar
60 ml (¼ cup) olive oil
1 small red onion, finely diced
175 g (1 cup) whole mixed olives
2 small tomatoes, diced
4 tablespoons finely chopped flat-leaf parsley
handful basil leaves, torn

Place the beans in a saucepan, cover with plenty of cold water and bring to the boil. Reduce the heat and simmer for 10 minutes, then turn off the heat and leave to soak for 2 hours.

Drain the beans and cover with fresh water. Prepare a bouquet garni by tying the parsley, thyme and bay leaf together with unwaxed cooking twine. Add it to the beans with the garlic cloves. Bring to the boil, reduce the heat and simmer for 1½–2 hours, or until the beans are tender, and adding more water as required; dried beans vary greatly in cooking time, so keep an eye on them.

Drain the beans well, discard the bouquet garni and garlic, and place in a mixing bowl. While the beans are still warm, add the vinegar, olive oil and onion, season with sea salt and toss gently to combine. Leave to cool.

Stir the olives, tomato, parsley and basil through, then pack into an airtight container for transporting. Chill until required, but serve at room temperature.

CELERIAC REMOULADE

SERVES 4–6

1 small celeriac, about 500 g
1 teaspoon salt (optional)
2 teaspoons lemon juice (optional)
1 tablespoon roughly chopped herbs, such as flat-leaf parsley, chervil or chives

REMOULADE
185 g (¾ cup) homemade or good-quality mayonnaise
2 tablespoons dijon mustard
2 tablespoons lemon juice or white wine vinegar
white pepper, to taste

Peel the celeriac, then cut into long thin julienne strips, either by hand, or using a mandoline if you have one. Taste the celeriac: if it's slightly bitter, toss it in a large bowl with the salt and lemon juice, set aside for 30 minutes, then rinse and dry well with paper towel. Place the celeriac in a large bowl.

To make the remoulade, put the mayonnaise, mustard and lemon juice in a small bowl. Season with sea salt and white pepper and whisk together. Add the remoulade to the celeriac strips and toss to combine well. Cover and refrigerate for 2–3 hours, or overnight, for the celeriac to soften slightly.

This salad will keep in an airtight container in the fridge for up to 3 days. Serve sprinkled with the herbs.

DESSERTS

GRILLED PINEAPPLE WITH CINNAMON SUGAR & MINT
page 170

CHERRY & CHOCOLATE DESSERT PIZZA
page 173

GRILLED PEACHES WITH MASCARPONE & CARAMEL SAUCE
page 174

BARBECUED PEARS WITH CINNAMON & HONEY CRÈME FRAÎCHE
page 176

GRILLED FIGS WITH ROSEMARY & POMEGRANATE RICOTTA
page 177

NECTARINES WITH CITRUS & KAFFIR LIME SYRUP
page 179

RUM-SPIKED BARBECUED BANANA BOATS
page 180

GRILLED PINEAPPLE WITH CINNAMON SUGAR & MINT

SERVES 8

1 pineapple, peeled, cored and cut lengthways into 8 wedges
8 bamboo skewers, soaked in cold water
1 tablespoon softened butter
140 g (¾ cup) soft brown sugar
2 teaspoons ground cinnamon
pinch of sea salt flakes
mint leaves, to serve

Thread the pineapple wedges onto the skewers.

Preheat a barbecue grill to medium and lightly grease with oil.

In a small saucepan, cook the butter and brown sugar over low heat, stirring until melted. Add the cinnamon and salt and mix well. Remove from the heat.

Brush the sugar syrup over the pineapple wedges and cook on the grill for 3–5 minutes on each side, until caramelised.

Serve hot on a platter scattered with mint leaves.

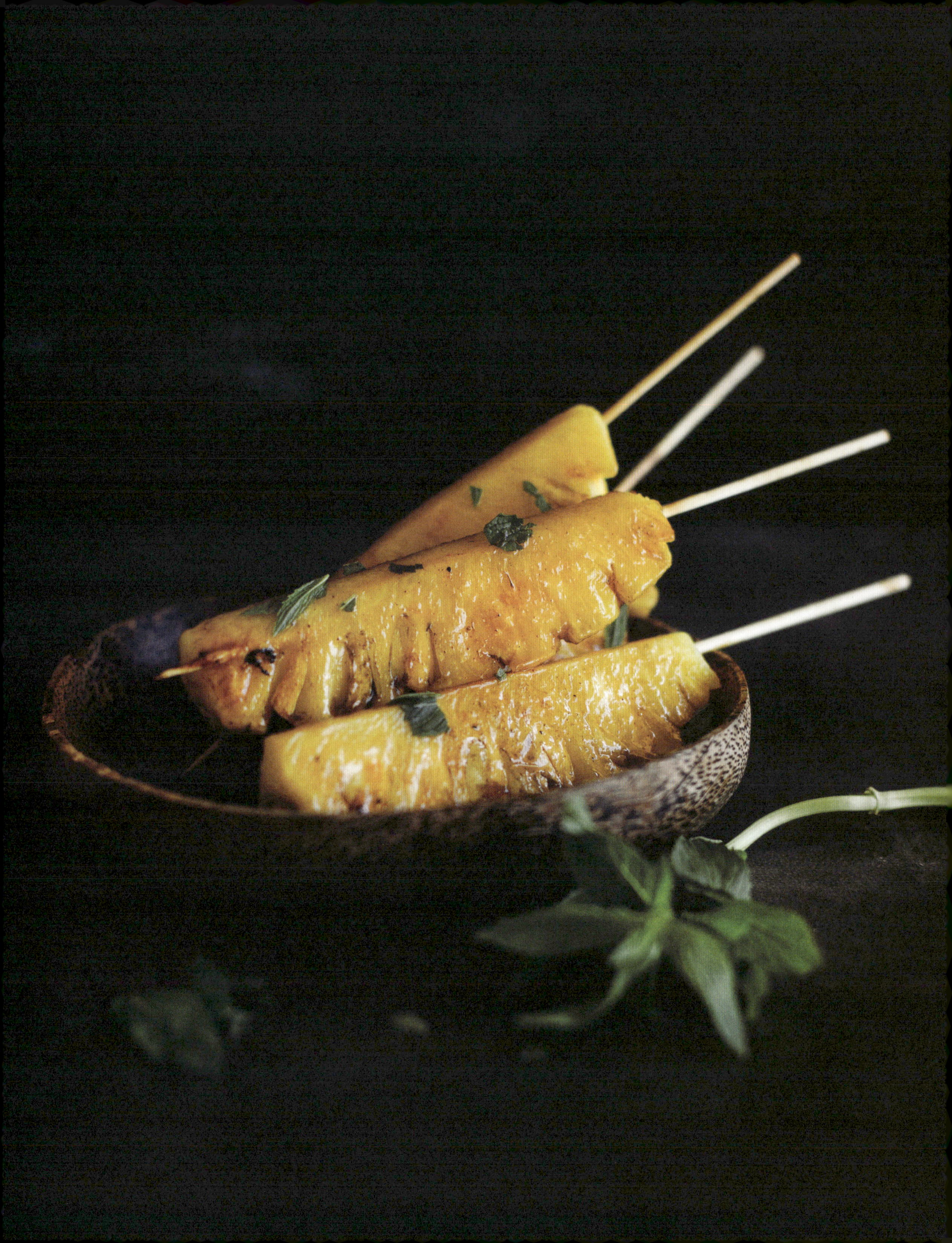

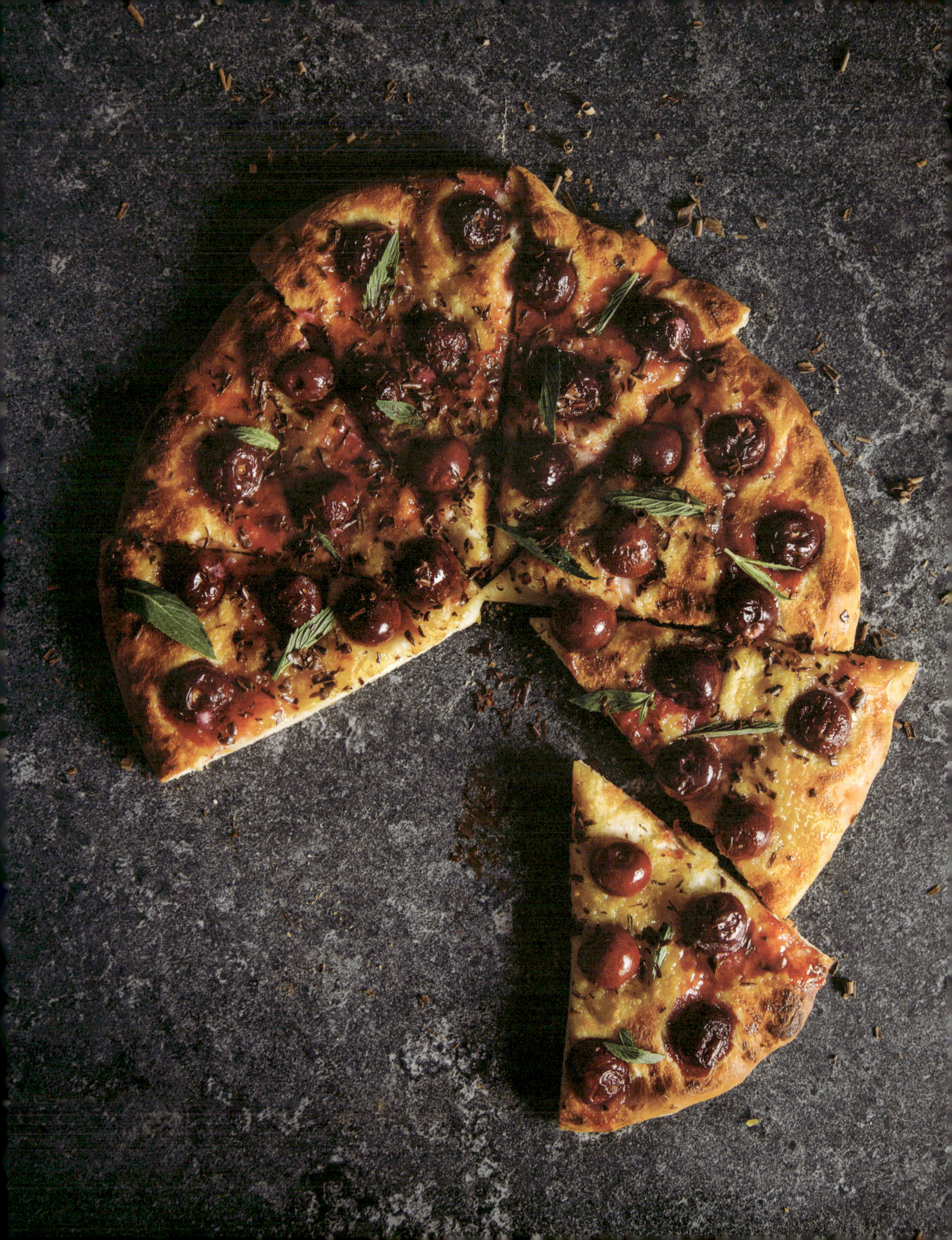

CHERRY & CHOCOLATE DESSERT PIZZA

SERVES 6

½ teaspoon active dried yeast
1 tablespoon caster sugar
1 tablespoon softened butter
80 ml (⅓ cup) warm milk
125 ml (½ cup) warm water
300 g (2 cups) strong flour
½ teaspoon sea salt flakes
50 g mascarpone cheese
2 teaspoons soft brown sugar
zest of ½ lemon
2 cups cherries, pitted
shaved dark chocolate, for topping
mint leaves, to garnish

In a large jug, combine the yeast, caster sugar, butter, milk and water and stir well. Set aside for a few minutes.

Place the flour and salt in a large mixing bowl and make a well in the centre. Pour the yeast mixture into the well and, using a spatula, draw the flour over the liquid to incorporate, until a dough forms. Tip onto a lightly floured work surface and knead the dough for 8 minutes until smooth.

Return the dough to the bowl and cover with a clean damp dish towel. Leave to rise in a warm place for 1 hour or until the dough has doubled in size.

Preheat a hooded barbecue grill to medium–high and lightly grease with oil.

Knead the dough again lightly to knock out the air. Roll out into a circle, about 25 cm in diameter, and place on a lightly oiled pizza tray.

In a small bowl, combine the mascarpone, brown sugar and lemon zest, then spread the mixture over the dough base. Arrange the cherries evenly over the top, lightly pressing into the dough.

Place the tray onto the grill, cover and cook for 15–20 minutes until the base is well cooked.

Remove from the heat and scatter with chocolate and mint leaves. Slice and serve.

Grilled Peaches with Mascarpone & Caramel Sauce

SERVES 4

35 g (¼ cup) whole hazelnuts
4 peaches, halved and stones removed
1 tablespoon softened butter
75 g (⅓ cup) mascarpone cheese

CARAMEL SAUCE
140 g (¾ cup) soft brown sugar
185 ml (¾ cup) cream
zest of ½ lemon

Preheat barbecue grill to medium low and lightly grease with oil.

Heat a frying pan over medium heat and toast the hazelnuts for 1–2 minutes until toasted and fragrant. Set aside to cool and then roughly chop.

To make the caramel sauce, combine the sugar with 60 ml (¼ cup) of water in a small saucepan over low heat, stirring until the sugar has melted. Use a wet pastry brush to brush down the side of the pan to dissolve any remaining sugar crystals. Bring to the boil and cook, stirring, for about 8 minutes until the mixture turns a light golden colour. Remove from the heat immediately. Set aside to cool for a few minutes then stir in the cream and lemon zest. The mixture may foam a little. Stir until smooth.

Brush the cut sides of the peaches generously with butter and place, cut-side down, onto the grill. Cook for 4–5 minutes or until grill marks appear.

Remove from the heat and serve immediately topped with mascarpone, caramel sauce and hazelnuts.

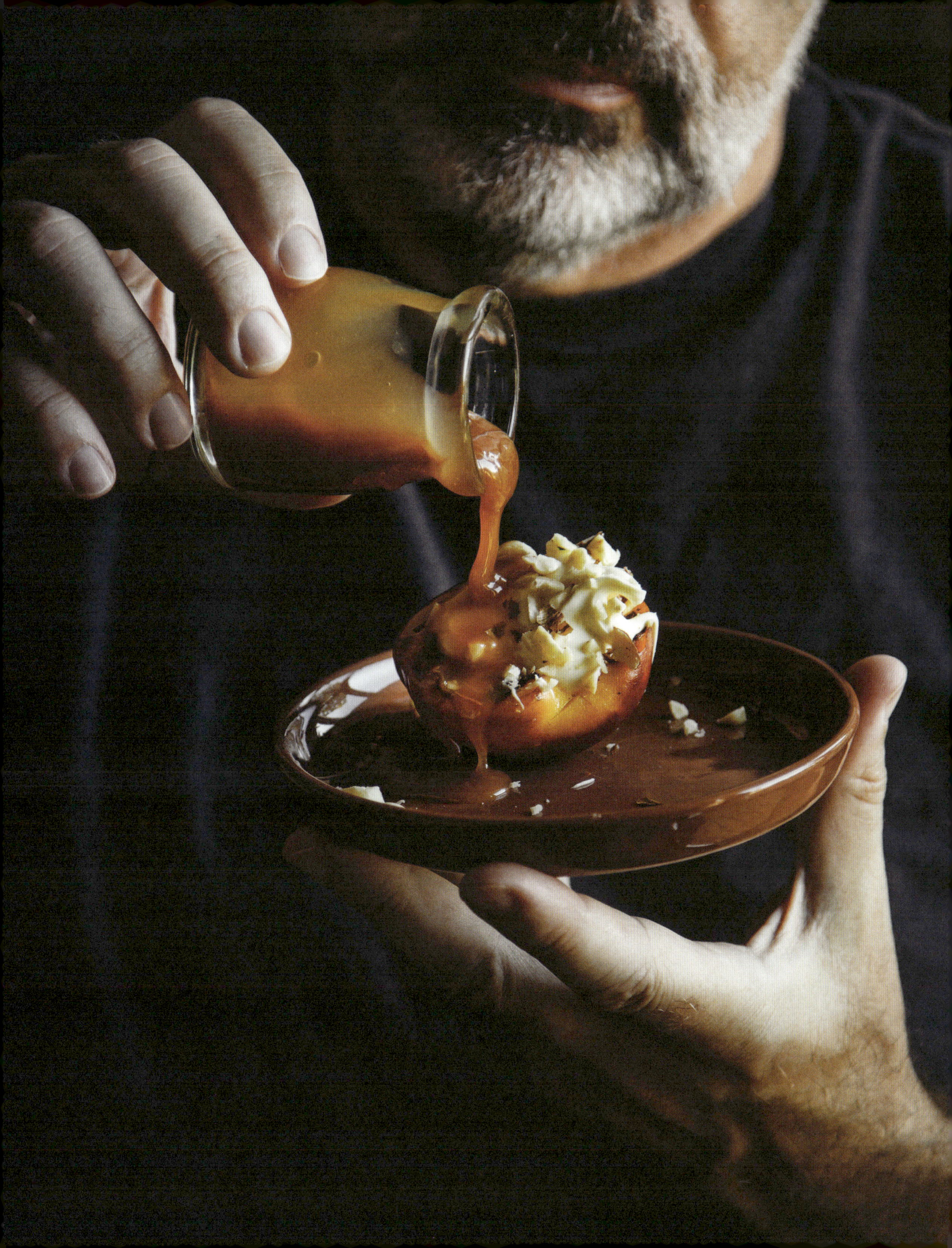

BARBECUED PEARS WITH CINNAMON & HONEY CREME FRAICHE

SERVES 4

4 firm beurre bosc or packham pears, cored, unpeeled
4 cinnamon sticks
125 ml (½ cup) honey
½ teaspoon ground cinnamon
100 g crème fraîche, to serve
thyme leaves, to garnish

Preheat a hooded barbecue grill to medium–low and lightly grease with oil.

Place a cinnamon stick in the hollowed core of each pear.

Wrap the pears in a double layer of foil and place on the grill. Cover and cook for 30 minutes.

Combine the honey and cinnamon with 125 ml (½ cup) of water in a small saucepan over low heat. Cook, stirring occasionally, for 5 minutes or until the syrup thickens slightly. Set aside to cool.

Unwrap the cooked pears and serve whole. Add a dollop of crème fraîche and spoon the cinnamon and honey syrup over the top. Garnish with thyme leaves.

GRILLED FIGS WITH ROSEMARY & POMEGRANATE RICOTTA

SERVES 4

200 g ricotta cheese

1 tablespoon pomegranate molasses, plus extra to serve

1 tablespoon lemon juice

1 tablespoon soft brown sugar

1 tablespoon finely chopped rosemary, plus extra sprigs to garnish

8 fresh figs, halved lengthways

25 g (¼ cup) walnut halves

Preheat a barbecue grill to medium and lightly grease with oil.

Heat a small frying pan over medium heat and toast the walnuts for 1–2 minutes until fragrant. Set aside to cool, then roughly chop.

Whisk the ricotta and pomegranate molasses together in a medium-sized mixing bowl.

In a small bowl, combine the lemon juice, sugar and rosemary. Stir to dissolve the sugar.

Brush the cut side of the figs with the lemon mixture, then place, cut-side down, onto the grill. Cook for 3–4 minutes or until grill lines appear and the figs are hot through.

Arrange the figs on serving plates with the ricotta and walnuts. Garnish with rosemary sprigs, and drizzle with a little extra pomegranate molasses.

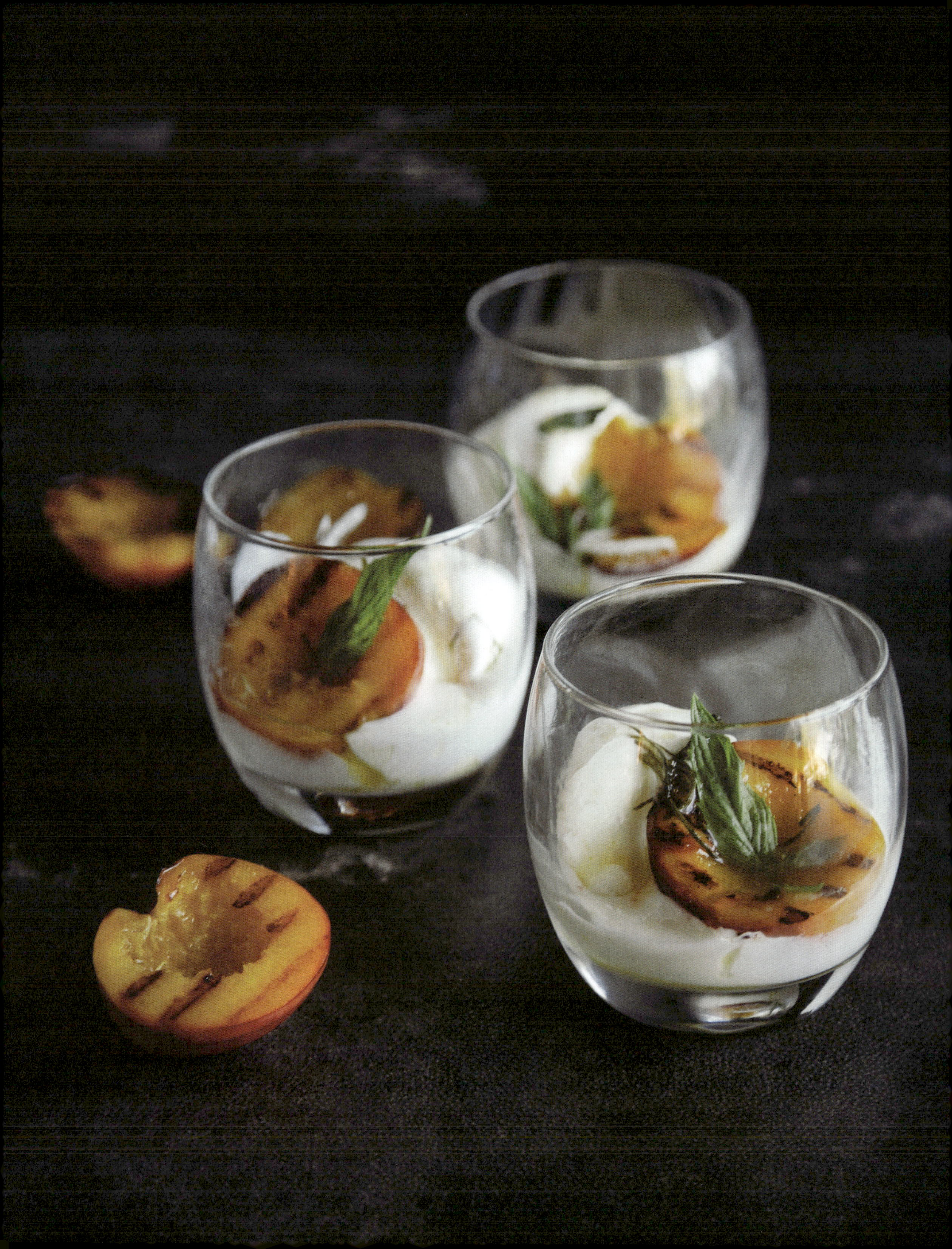

Nectarines with Citrus & Kaffir Lime Syrup

SERVES 4

4 ripe nectarines, halved and stones removed
1 tablespoon melted coconut oil
vanilla bean or coconut ice cream, to serve (optional)
mint leaves, to garnish

CITRUS & KAFFIR LIME SYRUP

230 g (1 cup) caster sugar
80 ml (⅓ cup) lime juice
60 ml (¼ cup) orange juice
1 tablespoon lemon juice
3 kaffir lime leaves, shredded
¼ cup mint leaves

To make the syrup, combine the sugar and the lime, orange and lemon juice with 80 ml (⅓ cup) water in a medium-sized saucepan over medium heat. Simmer until thickened and slightly syrupy. Add the kaffir lime and mint leaves and remove from the heat. Set aside for 20 minutes for the flavours to infuse.

Preheat a barbecue grill to medium–high and lightly grease with oil.

Brush the nectarine halves with coconut oil and grill for 3–5 minutes on each side until grill marks appear.

Strain the leaves from syrup. If the syrup has become too thick (it needs to pour), reheat gently and stir in a tablespoon of water.

Serve the nectarines with a scoop of ice cream (if you like) and a drizzle of the syrup. Garnish with mint leaves.

Rum-Spiked Barbecued Banana Boats

SERVES 4

4 bananas
60 g (⅓ cup) dark chocolate chips
20 g (¼ cup) shredded coconut, toasted
1 teaspoon ground cinnamon
2 tablespoons honey
2 tablespoons dark rum
vanilla bean ice cream, to serve (optional)

Preheat a hooded barbecue grill to medium and lightly grease with oil.

Using four pieces of heavy duty foil, shape a support for each banana by scrunching the foil up around the sides of the bananas, so they won't tip over while cooking on the grill.

Combine the chocolate, coconut, cinnamon, honey and rum in a small mixing bowl. Cut a slit into the bananas lengthways, leaving 2 cm intact at each end. Cut deeply, but not through the skin at the back. Divide the chocolate mixture between the bananas.

Place the bananas in their foil boats on the grill. Cover and cook for 4–5 minutes or until the skins have blackened and the chocolate has melted.

If you like, serve the bananas with a scoop of ice cream.

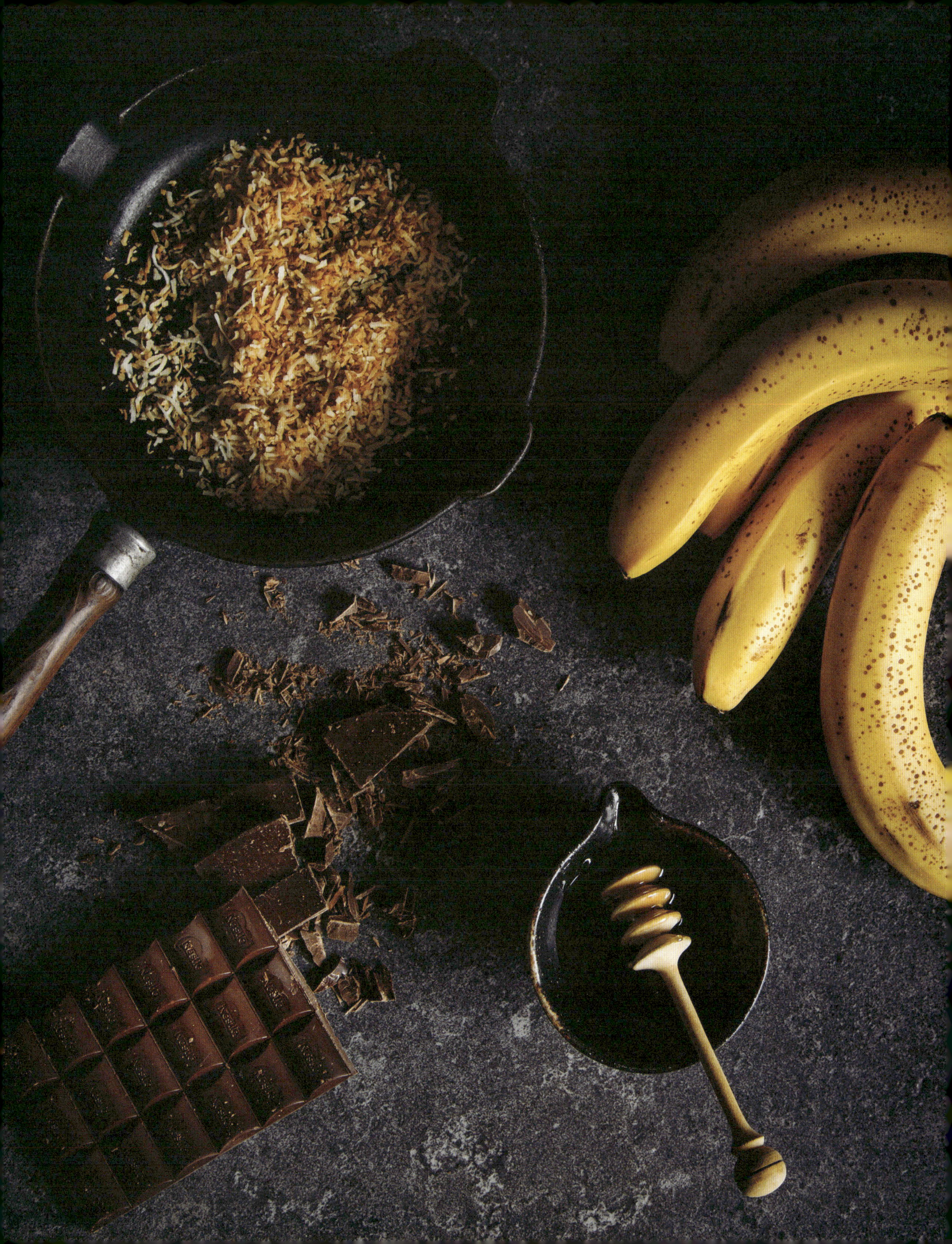

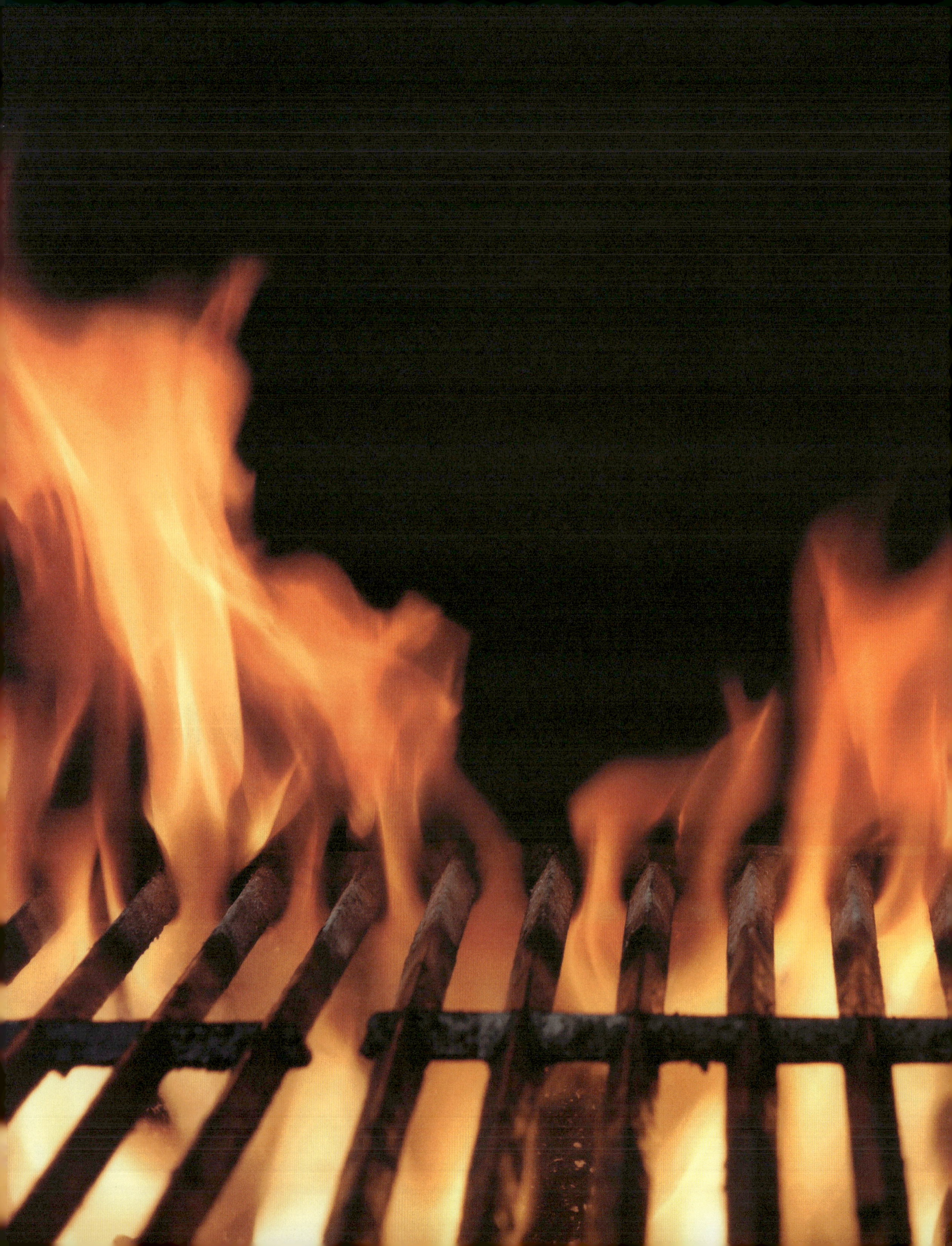

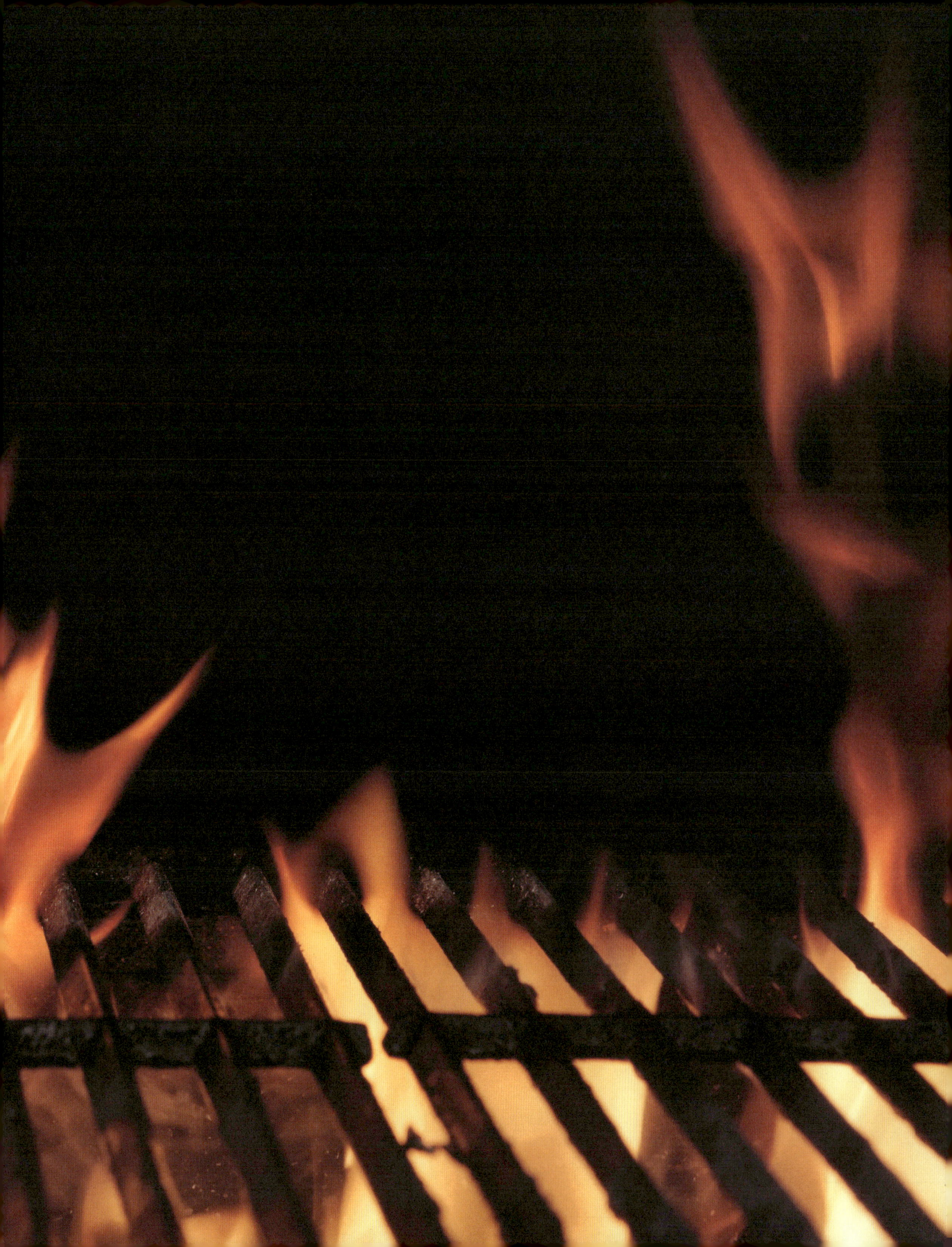

INDEX

A

Anchovy & Garlic Butter 85
Apple & Cabbage Slaw 144
Apple Cider Chicken Drumsticks 25
Apple Cider Marinade 25
Apple Sauce 118
Argentinian Beef With Chimichurri 101
Asparagus Wrapped In Bacon 42
Avocado, Feta & Dukkah, Baked Potatoes With 155

B

Baby Back Pork Ribs, Southern-Style 52
Bacon Skewers, Cherry Tomato & 43
Bacon Wrapped Mac & Cheeseburgers 55
Bacon–Weave Cheeseburgers 54
Bacon, Asparagus Wrapped In 42
Bacon, Kale & Jalapeño Salad, Fresh Corn, 146
Baked Potatoes With Avocado, Feta & Dukkah 155
Baked Potatoes With Cheese & Spring Onion Coleslaw 155
Banana Boats, Rum-Spiked Barbecued 180
Barbecue Sauce 52, 58
Barbecued Baked Potatoes 154–155
Barbecued Chicken Burgers With Basil Aioli 27
Barbecued Mediterranean Pizza With Basil Oil & Ricotta 129
Barbecued Pears With Cinnamon & Honey Crème Fraîche 176
Barbecued Peri Peri Chicken 18
Barbecued Potato Wedges With Lime Yoghurt 140
Barbecued Steak With Béarnaise Sauce 100
Basil Aioli 27
Basil Oil 129
Bbq Buffalo Wings With Blue Cheese Dip 32
BBQ Sauce, Bourbon-Laced 107
Bean Salad With Fresh Herbs, White 166
Béarnaise Sauce 98

Beef
Argentinian Beef With Chimichurri 101
Barbecued Steak With Béarnaise Sauce 98
Grilled Beef Fajitas With Salsa & Guacamole 111
Homemade Bratwurst 50
Homemade Pork & Veal Sausages 47
Rump Steak With Coriander & Jalapeño Butter 105
Sticky Beef Short Ribs With Bourbon-Laced BBQ Sauce 107
Thai Chilli–Coconut Surf & Turf Skewers 108
The Boss Beef Burgers 102
Veal Cutlets With Sage, Capers & Lemon 104

Beer Can Chicken, Tennessee 24
Blue Cheese Dip 32
Bourbon-Laced BBQ Sauce 107
Bratwurst, Homemade 50
Brazilian Cachaça Chicken Skewers 21
Buffalo Wings With Blue Cheese Dip, BBQ 32
Bulgogi Tofu, Korean 126

Burgers
Bacon Wrapped Mac & Cheeseburgers 55
Bacon–Weave Cheeseburgers 54
Barbecued Chicken Burgers With Basil Aioli 26
Edamame Burgers With Red Onion Jam 130
Haloumi Burgers With Peperonata 114
Lobster Tail & Salad Sliders 76
The Boss Beef Burgers 102
Burgers With Basil Aioli, Barbecued Chicken 27
Burnt Butter, Capers & Sage, Flounder With 70
Burritos, Chipotle Chicken 37
Butter, Coriander & Jalapeño 105
Butterflied Chicken With Rosemary Oil 31
Buttermilk Chicken, Grilled 22

C

Cabbage Salad, Grilled 164
Cabbage Slaw, Apple & 144
Cachaça Chicken Skewers, Brazilian 21
Cachaça Marinade 21

Calamari, Japanese Seven-Spice 73
Caper Aioli, Garlic & 69
Capers & Lemon, Veal Cutlets With Sage, 104
Capers & Sage, Flounder With Burnt Butter, 70
Caramel Sauce 174
Cauliflower & Sweet Potato Salad, Grilled 152
Cauliflower Steaks, Grilled Spiced 119
Celeriac Remoulade 167
Celery Remoulade, Crispy Skin Salmon With Fennel & 79
Chargrilled Witlof 145
Cheeseburgers, Bacon Wrapped Mac & 55
Cheeseburgers, Bacon-Weave 54
Chermoula 94
Chermoula Lamb Shoulder With Garlic & Tahini Yoghurt 94
Cherry & Chocolate Dessert Pizza 173
Cherry Tomato & Bacon Skewers 43

Chicken
- Apple Cider Chicken Drumsticks 25
- Barbecued Chicken Burgers With Basil Aioli 26
- Barbecued Peri Peri Chicken 18
- BBQ Buffalo Wings With Blue Cheese Dip 32
- Brazilian Cachaça Chicken Skewers 21
- Butterflied Chicken With Rosemary Oil 31
- Chipotle Chicken Burritos 37
- Fiery Lemongrass Chicken Wings 28
- Grilled Buttermilk Chicken 22
- Lemon & Garlic Wings 33
- Spicy Satay Chicken Skewers 34
- Tennessee Beer Can Chicken 24

Chilli-Coconut Marinade 108
Chilli-Coconut Surf & Turf Skewers, Thai 108
Chimichurri 101
Chipotle Aioli 37
Chipotle Barbecued Pork Ribs, Smokey 58
Chipotle Chicken Burritos 37
Chipotle Marinade 37
Chipotle Mayo 143
Chipotle Sauce 64
Chocolate Dessert Pizza, Cherry & 173
Chops With Preserved Lemon Gremolata, Lamb 93
Cider Chicken Drumsticks, Apple 25
Cinnamon & Honey Crème Fraîche, Barbecued Pears With 176
Cinnamon Sugar & Mint, Grilled Pineapple With 170
Citrus & Kaffir Lime Syrup 179
Coconut Surf & Turf Skewers, Thai Chilli- 108
Coriander & Jalapeño Butter 105
Corn On The Cob, Mexican 143
Corn, Bacon, Kale & Jalapeño Salad, Fresh 146
Crème Fraîche, Barbecued Pears With Cinnamon & Honey 176
Crispy Skin Salmon With Fennel & Celery Remoulade 79
Cucumber Salad 159
Currywurst 51
Cutlets With Sage, Capers & Lemon, Veal 104
Cutlets, Tandoori-Style Lamb 92

D

Desserts
- Barbecued Pears With Cinnamon & Honey Crème Fraîche 176
- Cherry & Chocolate Dessert Pizza 173
- Grilled Figs With Rosemary & Pomegranate Ricotta 177
- Grilled Peaches With Mascarpone & Caramel Sauce 174
- Grilled Pineapple With Cinnamon Sugar & Mint 170
- Nectarines With Citrus & Kaffir Lime Syrup 179
- Rum-Spiked Barbecued Banana Boats 180

Drumsticks, Apple Cider Chicken 25
Dry Rub 52, 58

E

Edamame Burgers With Red Onion Jam 130
Eggplant With Sage Oil, Grilled 150

F

Fajitas With Salsa & Guacamole, Grilled Beef 111
Fennel & Celery Remoulade, Crispy Skin Salmon With 79
Fennel Sausages, Homemade Pork & 46
Fiery Lemongrass Chicken Wings 28
Figs With Rosemary & Pomegranate Ricotta, Grilled 177

Fish & Seafood
- Baked Potatoes With Smoked Trout & Horseradish Crème 155
- Crispy Skin Salmon With Fennel & Celery Remoulade 79
- Flounder With Burnt Butter, Capers & Sage 70
- Grilled Tuna With Garlic & Caper Aioli 69
- Japanese Seven-Spice Calamari 73
- Lobster Tail & Salad Sliders 76

Louisiana Prawn Po'Boy 67

Prosciutto-Wrapped Scallops 75

Spiced Fish Tacos With Chipotle Sauce 64

Sugarcane Prawns 74

Thai Chilli–Coconut Surf & Turf Skewers 109

Whole Snapper With Thai Flavours 70

Fish Tacos With Chipotle Sauce, Spiced 64

Flatbread, Unleavened Grilled 137

Flatbread, Yeasted Grilled 136

Flounder With Burnt Butter, Capers & Sage 70

Fresh Corn, Bacon, Kale & Jalapeño Salad 146

Fritters With Apple Sauce, Potato 118

G

Garlic & Caper Aioli 69

Garlic & Tahini Yoghurt 94

Garlic Butter, Anchovy & 85

Garlic Lamb Kebabs With Quinoa Tabouli, Mint & 91

Garlic Wings, Lemon & 33

German Potato Salad 158

Greek-Style Slow-Cooked Lamb Roast 88

Gremolata, Lamb Chops With Preserved Lemon 93

Grilled Beef Fajitas With Salsa & Guacamole 111

Grilled Buttermilk Chicken 22

Grilled Cabbage Salad 164

Grilled Cauliflower & Sweet Potato Salad 152

Grilled Eggplant With Sage Oil 150

Grilled Figs With Rosemary & Pomegranate Ricotta 177

Grilled Lamb Loin With Anchovy & Garlic Butter 85

Grilled Peaches With Mascarpone & Caramel Sauce 174

Grilled Pineapple With Cinnamon Sugar & Mint 170

Grilled Pork Ribs With Vietnamese Dipping Sauce 49

Grilled Spiced Cauliflower Steaks 119

Grilled Tuna With Garlic & Caper Aioli 69

Grilled Vegetable & Haloumi Kebabs 117

Guacamole 111

H

Haloumi Burgers With Peperonata 114

Haloumi Kebabs, Grilled Vegetable & 117

Herby New Potato Salad 141

Homemade Bratwurst 50

Homemade Pork & Fennel Sausages 46

Homemade Pork & Veal Sausages 47

Homemade Tomato Ketchup 163

Hommus & Za'atar Grilled Vegetable Wraps 125

Hommus, Roasted Chickpea & Garlic 151

J

Jalapeño Butter, Coriander & 105

Jalapeño Salad, Fresh Corn, Bacon, Kale & 146

Jamaican Jerk Pork Belly 59

Japanese Marinade 73

Japanese Okonomiyaki 123

Japanese Seven-Spice Calamari 73

Jerk Marinade 59

Jerk Pork Belly, Jamaican 59

K

Kaffir Lime Syrup, Citrus & 179

Kale & Jalapeño Salad, Fresh Corn, Bacon, 146

Kashmiri Roast Lamb, Spicy 86

Kashmiri Spice Mix 86

Kebabs With Quinoa Tabouli, Mint & Garlic Lamb 91

Kebabs, Grilled Vegetable & Haloumi 117

Ketchup, Homemade Tomato 163

Korean Barbecued Pork 61

Korean Bulgogi Tofu 126

L

Lamb

Chermoula Lamb Shoulder With Garlic & Tahini Yoghurt 94

Greek-Style Slow-Cooked Lamb Roast 88

Grilled Lamb Loin With Anchovy & Garlic Butter 85

Lamb Chops With Preserved Lemon Gremolata 93

Mint & Garlic Lamb Kebabs With Quinoa Tabouli 91

Moroccan Lamb Meatballs With Minted Yoghurt 82

Rack Of Lamb With Rosemary Crust 87

Spicy Kashmiri Roast Lamb 86

Tandoori-Style Lamb Cutlets 92

Lamb Chops With Preserved Lemon Gremolata 93

Lemon & Garlic Wings 33

Lemongrass Chicken Wings, Fiery 28

Lemongrass Marinade 28, 34

Lime Yoghurt 140

Lobster Tail & Salad Sliders 76

Loin With Anchovy & Garlic Butter, Grilled Lamb 85

Louisiana Marinade 67

Louisiana Prawn Po'Boy 67

M

Mac & Cheeseburgers, Bacon Wrapped 55

Maple, Ginger & Orange Glaze, Pork Tenderloin With 40

Marinade, Chilli–Coconut 108

Mayo, Chipotle 143

Meatballs With Minted Yoghurt, Moroccan Lamb 82

Mexican Corn On The Cob 143

Mexican Quinoa Salad 161

Mint & Garlic Lamb Kebabs With Quinoa Tabouli 91

Minted Yoghurt 82

Mixed Mushroom Quesadillas 120

Moroccan Lamb Meatballs With Minted Yoghurt 82

Mushroom Quesadillas, Mixed 120

N, O

Nectarines With Citrus & Kaffir Lime Syrup 179

Nuoc Cham Dipping Sauce 74

Okonomiyaki, Japanese 123

P

Peaches With Mascarpone & Caramel Sauce, Grilled 174

Peanut Sauce 34

Pears With Cinnamon & Honey Crème Fraîche, Barbecued 176

Peperonata 114

Peri Peri Chicken, Barbecued 18

Peri Peri Sauce 18

Pineapple With Cinnamon Sugar & Mint, Grilled 170

Pizza Dough 129

Pizza With Basil Oil & Ricotta, Barbecued Mediterranean 129

Pizza, Cherry & Chocolate Dessert 173

Po'Boy, Louisiana Prawn 67

Pomegranate Ricotta, Grilled Figs With Rosemary & 177

Pork

Asparagus Wrapped In Bacon 42

Bacon Wrapped Mac & Cheeseburgers 55

Bacon–Weave Cheeseburgers 54

Cherry Tomato & Bacon Skewers 43

Currywurst 51

Fresh Corn, Bacon, Kale & Jalapeño Salad 146

German Potato Salad 158

Grilled Pork Ribs With Vietnamese Dipping Sauce 49

Homemade Bratwurst 50

Homemade Pork & Fennel Sausages 46

Homemade Pork & Veal Sausages 47

Jamaican Jerk Pork Belly 59

Korean Barbecued Pork 61

Pork Tenderloin With Maple, Ginger & Orange Glaze 40

Smokey Chipotle Barbecued Pork Ribs 58

Southern-Style Baby Back Pork Ribs 52

Pork & Fennel Sausages, Homemade 46

Pork & Veal Sausages, Homemade 47

Pork Ribs With Vietnamese Dipping Sauce, Grilled 49

Pork Tenderloin With Maple, Ginger & Orange Glaze 40

Portuguese Salad 149

Potato Fritters With Apple Sauce 118

Potatoes

Baked Potatoes With Avocado, Feta & Dukkah 155

Baked Potatoes With Cheese & Spring Onion Coleslaw 155

Baked Potatoes With Smoked Trout & Horseradish Crème 155

Barbecued Baked Potatoes 154–155

Barbecued Potato Wedges With Lime Yoghurt 140

German Potato Salad 158

Herby New Potato Salad 141

Prawn Po'Boy, Louisiana 67

Prawns, Sugarcane 74

Preserved Lemon Gremolata 93

Prosciutto-Wrapped Scallops 75

Q

Quesadillas, Mixed Mushroom 120

Quinoa Salad, Mexican 161

Quinoa Tabouli 91

R

Rack Of Lamb With Rosemary Crust 87

Ratatouille Parcels, Summer Veg 134

Red Onion Jam 130

Remoulade 67

Remoulade, Celeriac 167

Remoulade, Crispy Skin Salmon With Fennel & Celery 79

Ribs With Bourbon-Laced BBQ Sauce, Sticky Beef Short 107

Ribs With Vietnamese Dipping Sauce, Grilled Pork 49

Ribs, Smokey Chipotle Barbecued Pork 58

Ribs, Southern-Style Baby Back Pork 52

Ricotta, Grilled Figs With Rosemary & Pomegranate 177

Roast Lamb, Spicy Kashmiri 86

Roast, Greek-Style Slow-Cooked Lamb 88

Roasted Chickpea & Garlic Hommus 151

Rosemary & Pomegranate Ricotta, Grilled Figs With 177

Rosemary Crust, Rack Of Lamb With 87

Rosemary Oil 31

Rum-Spiked Barbecued Banana Boats 180

Rump Steak With Coriander & Jalapeño Butter 105

S

Sage Oil 150

Sage, Capers & Lemon, Veal Cutlets With 104

Sage, Flounder With Burnt Butter, Capers & 70

Salads

Apple & Cabbage Slaw 144

Celeriac Remoulade 167

Cucumber Salad 159

Fresh Corn, Bacon, Kale & Jalapeño Salad 146

German Potato Salad 158

Grilled Cabbage Salad 164

Grilled Cauliflower & Sweet Potato Salad 152

Herby New Potato Salad 141

Mexican Quinoa Salad 161

Portuguese Salad 149

Turkish Roasted Tomato Salad 162

White Bean Salad With Fresh Herbs 166

Salmon With Fennel & Celery Remoulade, Crispy Skin 79

Salsa, Fresh Tomato 111

Satay Chicken Skewers, Spicy 34

Sausages

Currywurst 51

Homemade Bratwurst 50

Homemade Pork & Fennel Sausages 46

Homemade Pork & Veal Sausages 47

Scallops, Prosciutto-Wrapped 75

Seafood, see Fish & Seafood

Short Ribs With Bourbon-Laced BBQ Sauce, Sticky Beef 107

Shoulder With Garlic & Tahini Yoghurt, Chermoula Lamb 94

Skewers, Brazilian Cachaça Chicken 21

Skewers, Cherry Tomato & Bacon 43

Skewers, Spicy Satay Chicken 34

Skewers, Thai Chilli–Coconut Surf & Turf 108

Slaw, Apple & Cabbage 144

Sliders, Lobster Tail & Salad 76

Slow-Cooked Lamb Roast, Greek-Style 88

Smokey Chipotle Barbecued Pork Ribs 58

Snapper With Thai Flavours, Whole 68

Southern-Style Baby Back Pork Ribs 52

Southern-Style Barbecued Tofu 124

Spiced Fish Tacos With Chipotle Sauce 64

Spicy Kashmiri Roast Lamb 86

Spicy Satay Chicken Skewers 34

Steak With Béarnaise Sauce, Barbecued 98

Steak With Coriander & Jalapeño Butter, Rump 105

Sticky Beef Short Ribs With Bourbon-Laced BBQ Sauce 107

Sugarcane Prawns 74

Summer Veg Ratatouille Parcels 134

Sweet Potato Salad, Grilled Cauliflower & 152

Sweet Recipes, see Desserts

T, U

Tabouli, Quinoa 91

Tacos With Chipotle Sauce, Spiced Fish 64

Tahini Yoghurt, Garlic & 94

Tandoori Marinade 92

Tandoori-Style Lamb Cutlets 92

Tennessee Beer Can Chicken 24

Thai Chilli–Coconut Surf & Turf Skewers 108

Thai Flavours, Whole Snapper With 68

The Boss Beef Burgers 102

Tofu, Korean Bulgogi 126

Tofu, Southern-Style Barbecued 124

Tomato & Bacon Skewers, Cherry 43

Tomato Ketchup, Homemade 163

Tomato Salad, Turkish Roasted 162

Trout & Horseradish Crème, Baked Potatoes With Smoked 155

Tuna With Garlic & Caper Aioli, Grilled 69

Turkish Roasted Tomato Salad 162

Unleavened Grilled Flatbread 137

V

Veal Cutlets With Sage, Capers & Lemon 104

Veal Sausages, Homemade Pork & 47

Vegetable & Haloumi Kebabs, Grilled 117

Vegetable Wraps, Hommus & Za'atar Grilled 125

Vegetarian
- Apple & Cabbage Slaw 144
- Baked Potatoes With Avocado, Feta & Dukkah 155
- Baked Potatoes With Cheese & Spring Onion Coleslaw 155
- Barbecued Mediterranean Pizza With Basil Oil & Ricotta 129
- Barbecued Potato Wedges With Lime Yoghurt 140
- Celeriac Remoulade 167
- Chargrilled Witlof 145
- Cucumber Salad 159
- Edamame Burgers With Red Onion Jam 130
- Grilled Cabbage Salad 164
- Grilled Cauliflower & Sweet Potato Salad 152
- Grilled Eggplant With Sage Oil 150
- Grilled Spiced Cauliflower Steaks 119
- Grilled Vegetable & Haloumi Kebabs 117
- Haloumi Burgers With Peperonata 114
- Herby New Potato Salad 141
- Homemade Tomato Ketchup 163
- Hommus & Za'atar Grilled Vegetable Wraps 125
- Japanese Okonomiyaki 123
- Korean Bulgogi Tofu 126
- Mexican Corn On The Cob 143
- Mexican Quinoa Salad 161
- Mixed Mushroom Quesadillas 120
- Portuguese Salad 149
- Potato Fritters With Apple Sauce 118
- Roasted Chickpea & Garlic Hommus 151
- Southern-Style Barbecued Tofu 124
- Summer Veg Ratatouille Parcels 134
- Turkish Roasted Tomato Salad 162
- Unleavened Grilled Flatbread 137
- White Bean Salad With Fresh Herbs 166
- Yeasted Grilled Flatbread 136

Vietnamese Dipping Sauce 49

W

White Bean Salad With Fresh Herbs 166

Whole Snapper With Thai Flavours 70

Wings With Blue Cheese Dip, Bbq Buffalo 32

Wings, Fiery Lemongrass Chicken 28

Wings, Lemon & Garlic 33

Witlof, Chargrilled 145

Y, Z

Yeasted Grilled Flatbread 136

Yoghurt, Garlic & Tahini 94

Yoghurt, Lime 140

Za'atar Marinade 125

Smith Street Books

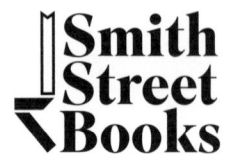

Published in 2017 by Smith Street Books

Melbourne | Australia
smithstreetbooks.com

ISBN: 978-1-925418-58-3

All rights reserved. No part of this book may be reproduced or transmitted by any person or entity, in any form or means, electronic or mechanical, including photocopying, recording, scanning or by any storage and retrieval system, without the prior written permission of the publishers and copyright holders.

Copyright recipes, text and design © Smith Street Books
Copyright photography © Billy Law

CIP data is available from the National Library of Australia

Publisher: Paul McNally
Senior Commissioning Editor: Hannah Koelmeyer
Recipe development: Sue Herold, Caroline Griffiths & Aisling Coughlan
Design concept: Kate Barraclough
Design layout: Heather Menzies, Studio31 Graphics
Photographer & Stylist: Billy Law

Printed & bound in China by C&C Offset Printing Co., Ltd.

Book 37

10 9 8 7 6 5 4 3

Please Note: recipes from this book have previously been published in *Feed The Man Meat*, published by Smith Street Books in 2016.